Emerging Pattern of Tribal Leadership in Arunachal Pradesh

Emerging Pattern of Tribal Leadership in Arunachal Pradesh

Dr. Rejir Karlo

Commonwealth

Emerging Pattern of Tribal Leadership in Arunachal Pradesh

Ist Edition : 2005
ISBN 81-311-0054-5

Published by :
Ajay Verma
For Commonwealth Publishers
4831/24, Prahlad Street,
Ansari Road, Darya Ganj,
New Delhi - 110002
Phone : 23272541, 23257835
Fax: 91-011-23257835
E-mail : campusbooks@hotmail.com

Laser Typesetting by :
Stylish Laser Typesetter
Delhi

Printed at :
Roshan Offset Printers
Delhi

To My Beloved
Wife Api

Preface

This work is the study of emerging pattern of grassroot leadership in Arunachal Pradesh in context of the rapid democratization of the tribal society. As the leaders are usually considered as precursor to change and development, this study highlights the complexities of the emerging situation. After the introduction of Panchayati Raj system and the emergence of multi-party competitive politics, the status and authority of the traditional village leaders have eroded to a great extent. Now, what we observe in the village is the emergence of multiple centres of power and conflicting decision-making process in the traditional village council. So, this study aims at comprehending the nature of transition taking place in the tribal polity and society.

At the completion of this work, I take the privilege to acknowledge my gratitude and indebtedness to Dr. P.K. Panigrahi, HOD of Political Science and Prof. A.C. Talukdar, former HOD of Political Science & Dean, Faculty of Social Sciences, Arunachal University for their able guidance and supervision. As teachers, they have always inspired and encouraged me towards academic pursuits. I owe my gratitude to numerous Gams, village elders, priests, panchayat members and other grassroot level leaders for their ready cooperation during the field study; to my colleagues in the Department of Political Science, J.N. College, Pasighat and the faculty members of the Department of Political Science, Arunachal University for their constant encouragement in my endeavour. I am also greatly indebted to some individuals like Marbi Kadu, Teluk Ragi, Tajen Dabi, Mado Doke, Ibom Doye, Ichak Lingu, Kenbom Karlo, Jumbom Gamlin, Topek Kakki and younger brother, Dabom Karlo, to name a few, for the help they rendered in visiting the field for collection of the data. My special thanks is also due to Dr. M.C. Behera, Reader, Department of Tribal Studies,

Arunachal University for his constant support and encouragement in my research work.

I owe my gratitude to the government of Arunachal Pradesh for granting study leave to enable me to complete this work; to the authorities and staff of all the libraries and institutions from where I collected materials for this study.

Without my wife Api and daughters Zirjum & Untu, this work would have been less rewarding. They are constant source of inspiration for me.

I am also grateful to Sanjoy Roy, Department of Botany, Arunachal University, who typed this work without a word of protest.

Finally, I admit that the limitations and errors in judgement in this work are entirely mine.

Rejir Karlo

Contents

1

Introduction

THE STUDY

To understand any political system, it requires an in-depth study of the existing patterns in a society. Leadership is one such aspect, which requires microanalysis to understand the socio-political system of a given society. Further, the leaders are usually considered as precursor to the change and development in the modern society.

Arunachal Pradesh is a late entrant into the modern democratic and representative politics. Prior to the introduction of the modern system of governance and administration, the traditional political institutions of respective tribes were the only forum for community decision-making and mechanism to regulate the society. Arunachal being a multi-ethnic society, the traditional political institutions were ethnic-specific. The deliberations in these tribal councils were guided by the traditionally influential village leaders and decisions were based on the customary laws of the land.

The *Gaon Burah* (popularly known as *Gam*) and other village elders played the leading role in the functioning of these councils. But with the introduction of statutory Panchayats and emergence of the competitive party politics, a new trend has emerged in the grassroots leadership pattern. This study is a micro-level attempt to understand the emerging leadership pattern in Arunachal Pradesh with specific reference to the Galo society—one of the ethnic groups in Arunachal Pradesh. Micro-research seems to be the need of the hour because "without the cluster of the micro-units the macro-unit can hardly perpetuate its consequential persistence. Seen differently, micro-level decisions, if remains non-implementative, threaten the very existence of the macro-system"[1]. The Galos have an elaborate and organized village council system known as *Keba* (popularly known as *Kebang*), an indigenous traditional political institution, responsible for taking care of issues involving socio-cultural development and conflict resolution. *Keba* being a democratic institution facilitates the participation of the members of the village without any discrimination. However, in practice, it is the village elders who are suppose to guide the proceedings of the *Keba*. It is observed that in Galo society, the *Gaon Burah* has been playing a significant role in the functioning of the *Keba*. In principle, a person with influence, knowledge of customary laws and acceptability in the village[2] was appointed as *Gaon Burah*. A person so appointed is recognized as village authority and empowered to try both criminal and civil disputes if the party is a resident within his jurisdiction. However, introduction of the statutory Panchayat and the emergence of competitive party politics have led to the emergence of the new type of leaders. The democratically elected Panchayat leaders are vested with the responsibilities of leading the rural mass towards the path of socio-economic development of the village. The party leaders are also becoming influential in the village affairs due to their linkage with the outside agencies. Unlike traditional leaders such as *Gaon Burahs* and village elders whose influence confined to their respective villages, the influence and link of the modern leaders are discernible across the village, clan and the tribe. Now, what we observe in the village is the emergence of multiple centres of power and decentralized decision-making authority; and in the process, the sole dominance of *Gaon Burahs* as leader of the village appears to be significantly eroded. Hence, in this study, an attempt

1. Tewary, I.N. (ed.), *Political System—A Micro-Perspective*, Anmol Publication, Delhi, 1986, p. 1.
2. See "Guidelines regarding appointment, power and functions of the Gaon Burahs", O/o Deputy Commissioner, East Siang District, Pasighat.

has been made to understand the emerging pattern of leadership in Galo society and to find out the relationship between the traditional and the modern leaders in terms of their determinants, attitudes, perceptions and so on. Further, the closed political system of the rural tribal society is usually vulnerable to the political manouvering on the basis of clan, family and the tribes. Hence, this study also looks into the importance and the extent of influence of the primordial loyalties in shaping the leadership pattern in Galo society.

REVIEW OF LITERATURE

Amidst complexities, the problem of leadership has attracted the interest of the scholars resulting into an impressive output of studies on the subject. But most of the studies on leadership give major emphasis on macro-study of the national and state level leadership. There are also abundance of literature on leadership in business enterprises and other formal institutions, which can hardly be related to the leadership process in the society or community. The studies on grassroot leadership too largely confined to leadership in the traditional context in village India only. The problem of leadership in context of the rapid democratization of rural society have not attracted as much attention of the scholars as they deserve and it is more so in the tribal societies. The present study, with main focus on the trend of leadership in the changing context, is a modest attempt to fill this gap. It would not be out of place to have a glimpse of few relevant studies on leadership.

In fact, D.S. Choudhary's *Emerging Rural Leadership in Indian States* (1981) is a scholarly attempt on the grassroot Panchayat leaders. He concluded that though there has been some visible change in the pattern of traditional leadership in rural India after the introduction of the Panchayati Raj institutions, the political power at the local level is still concentrated in the hands of rich peasantry and the people of higher castes which have traditional social status, wealth and many other strong points in their favour. Real democratization of power or involvement of the people of all sections of society is yet to take place[3]. Similarly, A.Y. Darshankar in his *Leadership in Panchayat Raj* (1979) observed, "Leadership is regarded as position of authority rather than one of service"[4]. But, S.N. Mishra in his *Political Socialization in Rural India* (1980) observed that there is sign of decentralization and diffusion of leadership between the upper caste and the lower castes[5]. The same author in *Politics and Leadership in Municipal Government* (1979) presented a vivid picture of dynamics of leadership in the urban and semi-urban areas. B.S. Bhargava in his *Grassroot Leadership* (1979) observed that the emerging leadership was individual-oriented and economic status was a powerful determinant of rural leadership, so 'the leadership cannot be called modern by any standard; at best it may be called neo-traditional'[6]. Writing about the traditional leaders among the Nagas, M. Horam in *Naga Polity* (1980) stated, "Good physique, dominating personality, eloquence in speech, bravery on the battle-field and kindness of heart are the prime requisite of a future leader"[7]. Bandyopadhyay (1985) cited the factors like introduction of Christianity, consolidation of British administration and extension of the relevant provisions of the Indian Constitution as reasons for what he termed 'leadership shift'[8] in the Mijo society. *Traditional Institutions of Meghalaya—A Study of Doloi and his Administration* (1988) by L.S. Gassah is a humble attempt to analyze the functioning of traditional tribal institution as it existed in the past and as it is today incorporating the

3. Choudhary, D.S., *Emerging Rural Leadership in an Indian State*, Manthan Publications, Delhi, 1981, pp. 117-118.
4. Darshankar, A.Y., *Leadership in Panchayati Raj*, Panchsheel Prakashan, Jaipur, 1979, p. 187.
5. Mishra, S.N., *Political Socialization in Rural India*, Inter-India Publication, Delhi, 1980, p. 142.
6. Bhargava, B.S., *Grassroot Leadership : A Study of Leadership in PRIs*, Ashish Publishing House, New Delhi, 1979, p. 62.
7. Horam, M., *Naga Polity*, B.R. Publishing Corporation, Delhi, p. 75.
8. Bandyopadhyay, P.K., *Leadership Among the Mizos*, B.R. Publishing Corporation, 1985, p. 233.

tradition, continuity and change. He observed that the new pattern of leadership reflects a transition from individual to collective, from the hereditary to elective and from ascriptive to achievement oriented. *Leadership in India* (1962) edited by L.P. Vidyarthi is one of the widely referred work on leadership. The first part of the volume deals with theoretical, methodological, as well as general traits of leadership in India. The second part is exclusively devoted to tribal leadership and the third part covers the various aspects of rural leadership. This volume is a commendable work to look at the problems of leadership in India in both the tribal and rural societies in the light of certain theoretical and methodological leads. But, most of these studies have been undertaken in different socio-political environment, which can hardly be related to the ongoing leadership pattern in Arunachal Pradesh in general, and Galo society in particular.

The work on leadership in context of the tribes of Arunachal Pradesh is very scanty. The existing works are mostly anthropological, sociological and on the history of the territory. Though there are certain works which address to the study of self-governing institutions of the tribes, most of them are based on observation, accounts and reports of the then British officers, narration by an individual, incidents and events, etc. Verrier Elwin's *Democracy in NEFA* (1965) gives a descriptive account of structural composition of almost all the tribal councils of Arunachal Pradesh. He cautioned against what he called 'Psychiatric Imperialism' which meant imposing new ideas of guilt and punishment on the tribal people[9] . J.N. Choudhury's *Arunachal Panorama* (1973) is a study of the profile of Arunachal Pradesh with major emphasis on the political evolution of the state. He also noted the impact of new forces on the traditional customs and institutions. Sanjay Dubey's *Dynamics of Tribal Local Polity and Panchayat Raj in Arunachal Pradesh* (1991) is also a study on the existing tribal councils of Arunachal Pradesh in the context of the introduction of statutory Panchayat. *The Wanchos* by Parul Dutta (1990); *A Tryst with*

9. Elwin, Verrier, *Democracy in NEFA*, Shillong, 1965, p. 27.

the Mishmi Hills by D.S. Negi (1996) are some of the recent publications on the tribes. But these works do not deal exclusively with the problem of leadership excepting some observations.

The Adis (erstwhile '*Abhors*') are relatively more studied among the tribes of Arunachal Pradesh due to their earlier contact with the Britishers and establishment of educational institutions relatively at an earlier date. *In Abhor Jungles* by A. Hamilton (1912), *Aspect of Padam-Minyong Culture* by Sachin Roy (1960), *Alluring Frontiers* by Tarun Kumar Bhattacharjee (1988); *History and Culture of the Adis* by T. Nyori (1993) and *British Relations with the Adis* by N.N. Osik (1992) are some of the important works on Adis which seek to trace the early and recent history of the Adis and gives significant informations about the indigenous socio-political institutions. A.C. Talukdar's *Political Transition in the Grassroots in Tribal India* (1987) sums up the trend of changes in the leadership pattern in the Panchayat perspective. But he devoted only a chapter on leadership, which gives an account of the transition in leadership pattern in Arunachal Pradesh with much emphasis on the *Kebang* of the *Padam-Minyong* group of Adis. Infact most of the works on the Adis are basically confined to the *Padam-Minyong* groups only. The present scholar has come across only two works, which exclusively deals with the Galos. The pioneering work on the Galos was carried out by L.R.N. Srivastava long back in 1962. His *The Gallongs* (1962) is a sociological work, which briefly gives an introductory idea of the Galos, their country, material culture, socio-economic organizations, rituals and few other aspect of their life. But, the author has not incorporated any dimension on leadership in his study except few observations on the political organization of the village. One commendable work on the Galo was done by B.B. Pandey entitled *Leadership Pattern in a Tribal Society* (1991). The study tries to provide a detail description of the traditional leadership pattern in the Galo society, which, hitherto, was neglected by earlier researchers. However, it is basically a sociological work, which tries to analyze the leadership pattern at the grassroot level of the Galo society with the help of the then Political Interpreter and Political

Jamadars. So, the study is little short of empirical discussion to assess the leadership pattern in real and emerging socio-political perspective. Further, long time has elapsed since these studies were conducted but the society under consideration is under rapid transition.

Thus, under the impact of the forces of modernization, an independent work on the grassroot leadership is yet to come up. More justification through participant observation and knowledge of local dialect to study the leadership pattern is urgently required. So, this study is a humble attempt by a local researcher to understand the emerging trends of leadership vis-à-vis political process at the grassroot level in Galo society.

CONCEPTUAL FRAMEWORK

The study of leadership has attracted the interest of the sociologists, political scientists and social psychologist alike due to the fact that it is an important aspect, which requires micro-analytical study to understand the political system of a given society. The growing complexities of life, advancement in science and technology, increasing role of government, rising expectation of the people and other similar factors have exalted the social significance of the study of leadership. But there is no unanimity among the writers and scholars as to what leadership actually mean? The studies on leadership conducted by different scholars under different socio-economic and political environments have produced different meaning and interpretation of the leadership. "The proliferation of research on leadership in cross-cultural context has enriched the concept but the plethora of ideas instead of reducing the complexities characterizing it has augmented it"[10]. It is aptly stated "leadership is one of the most observed and least understood phenomenon on earth"[11]. It is probably the most studied and least understood of any management subject[12]. There

10. Arora, K. Ramesh, in *Leadership* by G.P. Pilania, RBSA Publishers, Jaipur, 1999, pp. xxi-xxii.

11. Burns, James MacGregor, *Leadership*, Ambika Publications, New Delhi, 1978, p. 2.

12. Warren Bennis, as quoted in *Leadership* by G.P. Pilania, RBSA Publisher, Jaipur, 1991, p. x.

is a great variety of ways in which one individual stands out from others in social situation and in which the one may be said, therefore, to be leading the others. So diverse are these ways that "anyone concept attempting to encompass them all as 'leadership' does, loses the specificity and precision that is necessary for scientific thinking"[13]. "As social scientists have learned to probe beneath the manifest aspect of leadership and have been correspondingly more sensitive to the relevance of numerous and complex latent facts, they have found it more difficult to agree on what leadership is and does"[14]. Thus, leadership is a complex and ever-changing phenomenon depending upon the nature of situation, task and the group. But, even under these complexities, the scholars have tried to define and interpret leadership from different angle.

The word 'lead' comes from an Anglo-Saxon word, which means a road or a way; it is knowing what the next step is. So, leaders are those who lead or excel others in certain field and lead the group towards the desired goals. The leaders occupy a special position of influence in the group or society by virtue of certain individual personality traits, favourable situation and nature of the task to be accomplished. The Oxford English dictionary defines leaders as one who guides others in action or opinion; one who takes the lead in any business, enterprise or movement; one who is followed ..., a person of eminent position and influence. Thus, in a way, leadership is a process of leading, guiding and influencing others to accomplish certain goals. But the meaning and definition of leadership is not that simple. There is a lot of theoretical complexities due to the fact that variables like individual personality, situation and nature of the task to be accomplished together plays a significant role in the leadership process. Burns identified leadership with power when he says, "leaders are a particular kind of power holders. All leaders are actual or potential power

13. *International Encyclopaedia of Social Science,* Vol. 9, p. 91.

14. Choudhary, D.S., *Emergency Rural Leadership in An Indian State,* Manthan Publications, Delhi, 1981, p. 19.

holders but not all power holders are leaders"[15]. Thus, those who hold power are not necessarily leaders. The leaders enjoy certain degree of inner power to influence others in their action and opinion. But he influences the others out of consent, rather than of coercion. The followers cannot be forced to obey the commands of the leaders, but leaders are obeyed for the welfare of the led. There is symbiotic relationship between leaders and the followers because there can be no leading without following. So in the study of leadership phenomenon, the follower is as important as leader itself. M.N. Basu identified leadership in terms of "dominance, which include flattery, suggestion, argument, threat and physical forces"[16].

Basically there are three popular theories regarding the concept of leadership. Firstly, the trait theory, a traditional view of leadership, is still popular among many scholars. They tend to view the leadership as a special trait or set of traits or in-born qualities like initiative, courage, integrity, oratory and intelligence residing within an individual, which predestine him to be a leader. To them, leaders are born, not made. Ramesh K. Arora identified three principal traits of leadership as ABC, where A stands for Ability, B for Behaviour and C for Character[17]. All the attributes of leadership can be classified under these three traits, though relative importance of A or B or C would differ according to the environment in which leadership situation occurs. For that matter, various scholars have tried to identify different traits of leadership such as initiative, intelligence, foresight, enthusiasm, self-confidence, courage, loyalty, decisiveness, etc. D.R. Singh defined leadership as "a person who on the basis of certain qualities is accepted by the members of the group as superior; by virtue of which he occupies special status and position within the group; commands sufficient influence and control over the members of the group; and

15. Burns, James MacGregor, *Leadership* Ambika Publications, Delhi, 1978, p. 18.

16. Basu, M.N., *Role of Leaders in the Life of an Individual* in *Leadership in India* (ed.) L.P. Vidyarthi, Asia Publishing House, Delhi, 1962, p. 68.

17. See 'Introduction' of *Leadership* by G.P. Pilania, RBSA Publisher, Jaipur, 1991.

the members take pride in eulogizing his qualities by which they think he can lead the group towards goal fulfilment"[18]. The leaders especially in tradition-bound tribal society may owe their position to certain personality traits and characteristics such as known moral stand, knowledge about the traditional history and ability to deal with the issues. But the scholars and social scientists could not conclude with definiteness as to what characteristics are required for leadership and their attempt to isolate crucial traits of leadership have been proved abortive, as time and environment plays an important role in determining them.

Secondly, the modern psychologists and sociologists rejects the traits approach and instead give more emphasis on the interrelation of person and environment in studying the leadership phenomenon. Popularly known as situational theory, it maintains that leadership is a relationship that exists between persons in a social situation. To quote Murphy, "Leadership does not reside in a person. It is a function of the whole situation"[19]. Leadership is not symbolized by single individual, rather it rests in a fairly large number of persons thereby acquiring a plural character. Leadership is a relationship that exists between persons in a social situation, and persons who are leaders in one situation may not necessarily be a leader in other situation. Since leadership is a dynamic process depending upon situation, different situations need different kind of leadership. The individual who has particular trait or qualities required for a given situation will emerge as the leader in that particular situation. Thus, leaders are those who can respond more adequately to the needs of the situation or who can avail the given situation to lead the group towards the desired goal.

Thirdly, the Group Theory of leadership maintains that leadership is a functional relationship between three basic variables *viz.*, the leader, the group and the situation.

18. Singh, D.R., *Rural Leadership Among Scheduled Castes*, Chugh Publication, Allahabad, 1985, p. 13.

19. As quoted in *Social Change*, by Joseph K. Roucek, East-West Press Pvt. Ltd., Delhi, 1984, p. 288.

"Leadership is a concept applied to the personality-environment relation to describe a situation when a personality is so placed in the environment that his 'will, feeling and insight' direct and control others in the pursuit of a common cause"[20] (Pigor, 1935). Schnrich defines, "Leadership is a relationship between an individual and a group built around some common interest and behaviour as directed or determined by the leader"[21]. According to the International Encyclopedia of Social Sciences, "Leadership is a concept applied to the interaction of two or more persons when the evaluation of one or some of the parties to interaction is such that he or they come to the control and direct the actions of the others in the pursuit of common or compatible end"[22]. Thus, leadership is basically a function of personality and social system in dynamic interaction. It embraces a wide variety of interactional relationship, all of which have quite different effects in terms of group behaviour. Bernard M. Bass describes leadership as a "kind of interaction between or among people"[23]. To Fairchild, "Leadership is an act of organizing and directing the interests and activities of a group of persons ..."[24].

Besides, some scholars have identified leadership in terms of influence when it is said that 'leadership is the process of influencing collectively—a group of persons towards the achievement of specific goals[25]. Leadership is the 'activity of influencing people to cooperate towards some goal which they come to find desirable'[26]. Thus, this notion maintains that three variables such as leader, situation

20. As quoted in *International Encyclopaedia of Social Science*, Vol. 9, p. 22.

21. As quoted by V. Valini in *Rural Leadership in India*, Gian Publishing House, Delhi, 1991, p. 3.

22. *International Encyclopaedia of Social Science*, Vol. 9, p. 95.

23. Bass, B.M., *Leadership, Psychology and Organization Behaviour*, Harber & Row, New York, 1960, p. 19.

24. Fairchild, in *Dictionary of Sociology*, Totowa, Adams & Co., New Jersey, 1967, p. 174.

25. Pilania, G.P., *Leadership*, RBSA Publisher, Jaipur, 1991, p. 7.

26. Ordway Tead (1963), as quoted in *Rural Leadership in India*, by V. Valinia, Gian Publishing House, Delhi, 1991, p. 3.

and the group, influence each other thereby creating a leadership phenomenon.

In essence, each of the above-discussed conception of leadership taken separately reveals only a part of the total phenomenon. No particular definition and set of definitions can explain leadership in totality in exclusion of the others. All the approaches represent different facets of the same social phenomenon and yet they may not provide adequate theoretical framework for the study of leadership. But, it must be agreed that all the frameworks have their share of contribution to the study of leadership.

TYPOLOGIES OF LEADERSHIP

Attempts have been made by the scholars to categories the various types of leadership on the basis of different criteria of classification. On the basis of personality types and social roles, leaders have been classified as the political boss, the democrat, the bureaucrat, the diplomat, the reformer, the agitator and the theorist. On the basis of mode of exercise of their leadership, they have been classified as authoritarian, democratic and charismatic. On the basis of the relationship between the leaders and the led, they have been divided into institutional, dominant and persuasive leaders. Using the criteria of the origin of leadership, they have been classified as self-appointed, group-appointed and executive appointed leaders. And on the basis of the objectives of leadership, they have been categorized as executive leaders, intellectual leaders and artistic leaders. Merton (1957) has classified leaders into two categories—monomorphic and polymorphic on the basis of their area of influence. Leaders who wield their influence in a limited and small area are monomorphic, while those who exert influence in a number of areas are polymorphic. Burns (1978) has classified leadership into 'transactional leaders and transforming leader'[27] . The transactional leader carries on day-to-day routine business. He believes in non-interference. He is more a manager than a leader. The

27. Burns, James MacGregor, *Leadership*, Ambika Publications, New Delhi, 1978, p. 150.

transforming leader is vision-oriented, value shaper, path-finder, educator and a catalyst. His approach is always motivating, elevating, mobilizing, inspiring, uplifting and activating. Ayyangar pointed out three broad classification of leadership *viz.*, *(i)* those that are born leaders by their superior skills or ability, *(ii)* those that acquire leadership by consent of their followers or by the use of force, and *(iii)* those that have leadership thrust upon them[28]. While discussing the pattern of leadership, Nagpaul identified three types of leadership : *(a)* institutional leadership which refers to formal or appointive leaders who by virtue of their positions are expected to carry the leadership roles, *(b)* situational leadership which emerges at a time when institutional leadership is found to be inadequate, or informal leadership which commands respect and prestige in specific situation, *(c)* dictatorial or authoritarian leadership which tends to centralize all the functions in one individual and does not seek to evoke the maximum involvement of other members, and *(d)* democratic or creative leadership which promotes responsible participation by other group members and reinforces cooperative inter-personal relationship within the group[29]. However, it is not easy to compartmentalize various leadership types particularly the authoritarian and the democratic types because the totally democratic approach may not be easy to fit into well-established hierarchical form of organization, especially in traditional and transitional societies where non-democratic values are still held high. That's why Mishra (1979) added one more type called 'reality-oriented leadership'[30]. On the basis of the functions of leadership, Hamblin identified three types of leaders, *i.e.* task leader, procedural leaders and socio-

28. Ayyangar, M.A., *Tribal and Rural Leadership in India* in 'Leadership' (ed.) L.P. Vidyarthi, Asia Publishing House, Bombay/Delhi, 1968, p. 81.
29. Nagpaul Hans, *Leadership : A Frame of Reference* in 'Leadership' (ed.) L.P. Vidyarthi, Asia Publishing House, Bombay/Delhi, 1968, pp. 61-62.
30. Mishra, S.N., *Politics and Leadership in Municipal Government*, "Inter-India Publications, Delhi, 1979, p. 25.

emotional leaders[31]. The task leaders are more concern with groups' environmental problems. A procedural leader may influence the group the most in coordinating the activities of the various members into a cooperating whole. A socio-emotional leader may influence in helping group members to handle their emotions and maintaining group cohesion. But, there is always an overlapping of the functions as single individual may at the same time be the task, procedural and socio-emotional leader. On similar criteria of role, Gusfield also explains two types of leadership such as 'task leader and social leader'[32]. The task leader sets the condition of work performance and goal orientation. The social leader maintains the morale of the followers and the harmony of the social group. There is another type of leadership known as charismatic leaders. They are exceptional leader with exceptional individual personal qualities by virtue of which he is distinguish from common people. Max Weber said that charisma is often mixed with the traditional kind of authority. ...and that charisma depends not only on leader's qualities but also on the followers' receptivity[33].

However, the studies on tribal and rural society have produced a slightly different kind of leaderships, though above types are more or less equally applicable and identifiable in rural societies. In context of the emerging pattern of leadership in rural society, they may be classified broadly into traditional leaders and non-traditional leaders though no such dichotomous model of leadership necessarily exists. The traditional leaders are the village elders, chiefs, zamindars, feudals, etc. who are comparatively more caste-oriented, status quo-minded and individual oriented rather than institution-oriented. But such characterization of traditional leadership may not be always true in all societies

31. Robert L. Hamblin, *Leadership and Crisis in 'Leadership'* (ed.) L.L. Vidyarthi, Asia Publishing House, Bombay, 1968, p. 5.

32. Joseph R. Gusfield, *Functional Areas of Leadership in Social Movements* in 'Leadership' (ed.) L.P. Vidyarthi, Asia Publishing House, Bombay, 1968, p. 23.

33. As quoted in *Leadership in Panchayati Raj* by A.Y. Darshankar, Panchsheel Prakashan, Jaipur, 1979, p. 13.

particularly in some tribal societies where there are no social stratifications. They are the leaders who are legitimately accepted in the society or village on the basis of their capability, sense of justice, experience, knowledge about traditional codes and their cooperative attitude in solving the problems. The non-traditional leaders are modern institutional leaders who perform routine functions of their status allotted to them in the society. In our study, they are democratically elected members of the representative institution of Panchayat bodies. Besides these, we may add another type of leadership called transitional leaders who attained the leadership in the traditional manner but through their contact with the other world have acquired comparatively newer ideas and aspirations. Mishra (1980) found two types of leadership in Bihar Panchayat bodies : upper middle class leadership and lower class leadership. Till the introduction of the statutory Panchayat, influential members of the Bhumihar caste used to become the headman of the village but the introduction of statutory Panchayat has made a substantial difference on the domination of Bhumihars in the village affairs. There is a change in the attitude of traditional leadership, and the traditional leadership is gradually receding in the background[34] . Sahay (1981) has pointed out that there are three types of leadership in tribal society—*(a)* traditional leaders such as village or regional headman, sacred specialist, traditional medicine man, and so on, *(b)* emergent leaders like Mukhya, Sarpanch, Chairman, etc. and *(c)* traditional-emergent leaders such as erstwhile traditional leaders who are trying to swim with the new currents. According to Bhouraskar, the indigenous leadership of the village could be classified into two categories namely 'official and non-official leaders. Non-official village leadership could be further classified into two : formal and informal'[35] . The formal leadership is attributed to governments position and

34. Mishra, S.N., *Political Socialization in Rural India*, Inter-India Publications, Delhi, 1980, pp. 101-102.

35. Bhouraskar, K.N., *Dynamics of Leadership in a Tribal Village*, in 'Leadership' (ed.) L.P. Vidyarthi, Asia Publishing House, Bombay, 1968, p. 203.

formal institutions. Bandyopadhyay called them as 'positional leaders occupying formal position in organizations and use the position as sets of tools in the process of power or pattern of interaction where power is distributed'[36]. The informal leadership may or may not be traditional. It includes influential persons in the village. They may not occupy any formal position, but can take decisions on behalf of the villagers and influence the decisions. They are the real leaders of the community and voice the group's collective conscience.

The general overview of the studies on leadership in the tribal and rural society clearly indicates the emergence of a new type of leaders to whom many scholars prefer to call the 'modern' leadership. They are comparatively younger leaders with some educational background, having wider area of influence because of their regular contact with the government officials and other outside agencies. One of the best examples is the representative of the Panchayat bodies who are democratically elected leaders. In nutshell, the modern leadership has got achieved status rather than ascribed. But Rangnath was cautious enough when he said, "it is no wonder that in certain important levels of rural leadership some of its traditional determinants like the higher caste status are still powerful. In this way, the evolving pattern of rural leadership presents a picture of an amalgam of new trends and traditional elements though it is evident that the older forces appear to fight a losing battle"[37]. Bhargava also preferred to call them as 'neo-traditional'[38] instead of modern leaders. Such views on the emerging types of leadership are also not out of place especially in the context of the tribal and caste-ridden rural society in India. Certain status symbols tend to persist in

36. Bandyopadhyay, P.K., *Leadership Among the Mizos*, B.R. Publishing Corporation, Delhi, 1985, p. 85.

37. Rangnath, *Rural Leadership : Old and New* in 'Leadership in India' (ed.) L.P. Vidyarthi, Asia Publishing House, Bombay, 1968, p. 275.

38. Bhargava, B.S., *Grassroot Leadership : A Study in PRIs*, Ashish Publishing House, New Delhi, 1979, p. 62.

spite of shifts in the centre of effective authority and leadership[39].

LEADERSHIP IN ARUNACHAL PRADESH

Arunachal Pradesh is the late entrant into the modern representative politics. Prior to the advent of the British in the region, this land was almost unknown to the other parts of the country. The interaction with the Ahom administration was very occasional and casual. There was no formal rules and regulations to govern the society except the traditional political institution of each tribe. The society was regulated through the traditional political institutions, now popularly known as village councils. These village councils have managed to serve as an effective dispute resolution mechanism, thereby maintaining the harmony and cohesion in the society. Apart from the judicial decisions, the village council is concerning with all activities related to the welfare and security of the village. The striking feature of the functioning of village councils in Arunachal Pradesh is the role of elders as its leaders. The elders are informal leaders who by virtue of their wisdom, knowledge, wealth and other similar traits have significant influence in the village in terms of decision-making. Their word is always respected and obeyed by the common people. The age and wisdom has special place in the leadership structure of almost all the tribes of Arunachal Pradesh. Thus, the tribal council is basically a council of elders. In the traditional context, different tribes have different nomenclature for the institutional village leaders though their role is more or less similar, if not identical. The *Tsorgen* of the Monpa is the chief not by birth but by unanimous election/selection by the Monpa village council known as *Tso-Tsangzom.* In addition to the power conferred on him by the Assam Frontier (Administration of Justice) Regulation of 1945, the *Tsorgen*, in the capacity of village authority, is competent to decide all civil and criminal cases under the customary law. His duties include not only the administration of the village but

39. Roy Burman, B.K., *Changes in Leadership Pattern* in 'Leadership in India' (ed.) L.P. Vidyarthi, Asia Publishing House, Bombay, 1968, p. 235.

also giving advice and guidance in all matters concerning its welfare as a whole and of any individual householder. Each household renders one-day service to the chief (*Tsorgen*) annually or pays equivalent amount in cash or kind, which signifies the authority, legitimacy and the respect he commands in the society. The *Tsorgen* is always assisted in his works by *Gomin* (messenger) and the *Tsoblas* who represent him in different villages. The *Tsoblas* can also try the petty cases with the help of panel of assessors known as *Mangma*. The village council of the Sherdukpen is known as *Jung*, which consists of village headman (*Thik akhao*), other members of the council (*Jung me*), a courier and a chowkidar. The official *Gaon Burah* also plays a prominent role in the functioning of the village council but any decision in the village must respect or conform to the consensus of the public opinion. The persons of importance in Aka village council (*Mele/Raiz*) are the *Gaon Burah*, the *Borah*, and the *Gibba* who commands an influence in the village by virtue of their position. Besides them, the elder people of the community have also say in the matters. Respect is usually given to age. "Apatani villages lack a centralized authority wielding power over all the inhabitants, but village affairs are managed in a somewhat informal manner by a council of clan representative called *Buliang*"[40]. There are three types of Buliangs. The Aka Buliangs are the principal leaders of age and wisdom who are always consulted on all important matters. The Yapa Buliangs are more dynamic leaders of middle-aged men who practically take the decision and settle the dispute. But, practically there is overlapping of duties. The *Ajang Buliang* consist of young men who act as messengers and assistants to the *Yapa Buliang*. "Though the *Buliangs* are collectively the upholders of tribal law, they act primarily as the spokesman of their own clan or clan group, and not as village headman invested with absolute authority"[41]. Their duties are those of arbiters rather than of the judge. The village council (*Abbala*) of the Idu Mishmi tribe usually composed of a few

40. Elwin, Verrier, *Democracy in NEFA*, Shillong, 1965, p. 81.

41. *Ibid.*, p. 82.

elderly villagers reputed for their wisdom and soundness of judgement. The political authority of the Khamptis vests in the village chiefs who normally belong to one of the royal classes. The office of the chief is hereditary in clan only, not in the family. But the chief exercise his authority through a council (*Mokchup*), the member of which is recruited from the people of various social statuses. The village council of the Nockte (*Ngothun*) consists of the chief as its head and few other elderly experienced members. The chief though seems authoritarian always consult the council. The chief is assisted by other functionaries like—*Ngongba, Ramba, Tamba, Kampa* and the official *Gams*. In each Wancho village, there is well-organized 'council of elders' known as *Wanchu-Wangcha*. The '*Wangham*', chief, is the head and he is assisted by number of designated members with different functions. The number of members and their functions vary from village to village. The Tangsas have also well organized council of elders known by different names in different sub-tribes such as *Khaphua, Khapong, Khapo* and so on. These councils consist of leaders who are appointed on the basis of their wealth and intelligence, and the other members represent the various clans.

Apart from the positional institutional leaders of the various tribes, there are other leaders who are equally, if not more, influential in the society. The first categories of such leaders are the prominent elders of the village. In each village council, the elder people have special position though they do not hold any formal position in the traditional socio-political structure. In tribal councils, the age and wisdom has special place. Such people are always obeyed and consulted in arriving at a decision. Secondly, the *Gam* or *Gaon Burah* plays a prominent role in the functioning of the village council especially in those issues, which concern with the award of justice and punishment according to the customs and the conventions. His status as village leader is further elevated due to the rapport he enjoy with the administration. In principle, an elderly responsible person whom the people consider as their legitimate leader in the village is usually appointed as *Gam* by the district administration and he is provided with red coat as status symbol. He is paid annual honorarium by the government according to the seniority in the service. Hence, they are the official leaders who link the village with administration, especially for correspondence and other judicial decisions. Thirdly, the introduction of Panchayati Raj in 1967 coupled with the emergence of multi-party competitive politics have opened up new avenues for comparatively younger people to assume the leadership roles. The emerging new leaders of the Panchayat bodies and the political parties are supposed to be more adaptive to the changing tune of the time. The changing context has necessitated a new trend in the leadership phenomenon. The leadership is becoming more formal and likely to be more scattered. The traditional pattern of group leadership is being gradually replaced by individualistic, semi-official and artificate leadership[42]. It is also observable that with changed scenario, the rural leadership is becoming more broad based and party politics is augmenting the enlarged role of the modern institutional leaders.

LEADERSHIP IN THE GALO SOCIETY

The village council (*Keba*) of the Galos, which is popularly known as *Kebang* do not recognize single individual or a separate body of individuals as the ultimate authority in the village. The Galos, who are popularly considered as one of the major sub-tribe of the Adis[43], have similar system of village council with that of the other Adis. All the adult members of the village are the natural members of the council (*Keba*) and they are free to participate in the proceedings and meetings. The Galo village has got collective leadership. No single individual is as influential as to dictate or dominate the decisions of the *Keba*. The traditional leadership structure is not hereditary or ascribed as in some other tribes. "In practice, however, many of the proceedings of such meetings concern only a few of the members present,

42. See 'Introduction', "Leadership in India" (ed.) L.P. Vidyarthi, Ashish Publishing House, Delhi, 1968.
43. Some sections of the Galos who are based in urban areas are claiming Galo as separate tribe different from the Adis. But, such opinion is yet to get a social approval.

those who have sufficient knowledge of the subject under consideration or those who are well-versed with the intricacies of the tribal law. Thus, the expert plays their part while others only sit and listen. But in the matter of judgement, it is the consent of the village community in its corporate capacity that largely counts"[44]. The men of age, wisdom, experience, and knowledge about customary laws have got special status in the decision-making process. On Adi leadership, Tarun Kumar Bhattacharjee wrote, "Gifted with knowledge of myths and customs they carried a great deal of conviction with the audience while expressing a thought. They were extempore speakers, voice rise in a crescendo while elaborating a point on customary law and belief of forefathers since the days of *Pedong Nane*—the mythical mother of all beings"[45]. "An important characteristic of the leadership pattern in most of the village councils was that it was not instantaneous but a result of tortuous and prolonged process of acquiring mastery over a large corpus of customs and jurisprudence and gaining confidence of the fellow villagers. But in all cases, the leaders had to gain recognition through their age, knowledge of customary laws, years of experience and proven ability through their sustained interest and active participation in the public affairs"[46]. Thus, the ultimate decision is taken by the village elders popularly known as *Kebang Abu/Keba Abo*. Here, the *Keba Abo* are the village elders who do not occupy any formal position but take leading role in the judicial decisions and other community affairs in the village. The terms frequently used to designate such prominent village elders of the Galo society are *Nyijik*, *Nyikok* and the *Rutum*. The spiritual leader like priest is known as *Nyijik* or *Nyibuh* or *Jikte* according to their status. The prominent priest (*Jikte*) is usually invited to distant villages also. They (*Nyijik* or *Jikte*) are the spiritually gifted people who are

44. Elwin, Verrier, *Democracy in NEFA*, Shillong, 1965, p. 71.

45. Bhattacharjee, T.K., *Alluring Frontiers*, Omsons Publications, Gauhati/Delhi, 1988, p. 207.

46. Talukdar, A.C., *Political Modernization in Arunachal Pradesh*, in 'Sequences of Development' (ed.) J.B. Bhattacharjee, Omsons Publications, Delhi, 1989, p. 98.

believed to have acquired the power to communicate with different benevolent and malevolent spirits and deities. Such people are rarely available. They are the medium of communication or only link between the human being and the supernatural powers. They are born, not made or acquired. The *Nyikok* symbolize the person who has deep knowledge of traditions, conventions, practices and customary laws coupled with good oratorial skills, interpretation, analysis and judgement. The dividing line between the *Nyikok* and the *Rutum* is very narrow, if not non-existent. "*Rutum* is one who is known to be public-spirited and take an active part in all activities of public welfare"[47] . But, apart from other individual personality, the *Rutum* is influential because of wealth or economic status and his ready generosity on the public occasions. "It should, however, be remembered that these are not public offices as such. They indicate personal status and prestige the persons acquired in public estimation on account of their talents, merits and achievements"[48] . These people are neither elected nor formally selected, rather, they are accepted by virtue of their talent, knowledge and wisdom.

The British penetration into the region was fraught with far-reaching effects of great magnitude especially in the leadership structure of the traditional society. The system of appointing *Gam/ Gaon Burah*, Political Interpreter, and Political *Jamadar* was a totally new innovation for the Galos and other tribes alike. Under the Assam Frontier (Administration of Justice) Regulation of 1945, the age-old authority of village councils, headmen and the chiefs, wherever existed, were formally recognized as village authorities and vested with the task of maintaining peace and order within their jurisdiction. Some prominent and influential village elders (*Keba Abo*) were spotted and appointed by the administration as *Gam* thereby created positional/formal leaders in the village *Keba*. They were provided with 'red coat' to symbolize the formal authority

47. Pandey, B.B., *Leadership Pattern in a Tribal Society*, Spectrum Publication, Delhi/Guwahati, 1991, p. 56.

48. *Ibid.*, p. 57.

given to them and the system still continues. Now, a *Gaon Burah* has authority because he is in the office. Initially, they were not paid but now-a-days the *Gams* are paid an annual honorarium. Another class of influential people invested with formal authority in the grassroot level was the Political *Jamadar* and the Political Interpreter. The Political Interpreter, as its name suggests, was appointed merely as translators and conveyors of the decisions and orders of the government to the people. The village people could convey their prayers and appeals to the officers through the interpreters only. They were paid officials of the British government. But the very nature of their job such as close association with the officers and knowledge about the formal rules and officials procedures made them popular in the eyes of the innocent villagers. Hence, they became instrumental in settling the disputes and awarding compensation to the victims. The Political *Jamadar* was also a paid government personnel. He was a substitute for regular Area Superintendent in the places and area where such official was not posted. The *Jamadar* was practically drawn from the local people only. Thus, the system of appointing *Gam*, political interpreter and the Political *Jamadar* introduced 'individual authority in place of the community authority'[49] because these personnel were practically super-imposed by the government without necessary consent of the public. The official interference in the community administration led to the cracks in the traditional leadership structure. The imposition of statutory organ in the customary institution (*Keba*) has led to the gradual degeneration of village democracy and its leadership. Thus, the *Gam*, Interpreter and the *Jamadar* were the first group of people in the Galo society who were conferred with formal authoritative position of influence in the villages. Dr. B.B. Pandey rightly described them as 'official leadership'.

Another round of transformation in the leadership process in Galo society took place with the introduction of Panchayati Raj in 1967 AD and the subsequent elections to various posts of the Panchayat bodies. This ushered, at least

---

49. *Ibid.*, p. 63.

in principle, into an emergence of formally and democratically elected leaders drawn from comparatively younger generation. These emerging leaders of the Panchayat bodies become instrumental in the decision-making process relating to the developmental programmes and the developmental priorities. Hence, the corporate authorities of the village under the guidance of traditional leaders are shared by the new modern leaders of the Panchayat bodies. Besides the Panchayat bodies, the emergence of party politics has brought about further transformation in the leadership process in the Galo society in form politicization of the village community and the legitimatization of the majority decisions. The Panchayat has been instrumental in bringing the party politics to the villages.

OBJECTIVES OF THE STUDY

To make the study of leadership more meaningful, it must be viewed in context of changes taking place in the society. Thus, this study revolves around the following major objectives :

(1) To analyze the socio-economic background of both the traditional and the modern leaders and thereby understand the emerging pattern of leadership.

(2) To understand the attitude, perceptions and orientation of the traditional and the modern leaders respectively.

(3) To analyze the decision-making process in the village in light of the rapid democratization of the rural society and the emerging pattern of leadership.

(4) To study the role of primordial loyalties in the leadership process.

HYPOTHESES

This study have tested the following hypotheses :

(1) The leadership pattern in tribal society is undergoing a process of change due to the impact of political modernization. The modern leadership is becoming more popular than the traditional leaders. But,

recruitment to leadership is not that democratic as it is generally thought of.

(2) The attitudes and perceptions of the leaders are in tune with the changing socio-political environment.

(3) The decision-making process at grassroot level is now marked by conflict and competition. Authoritarian and arbitrary decisions are not uncommon.

(4) Though democratic norms have entered into the political process in the tribal society, the primordial loyalties determine the recruitment of leadership to a great extent.

METHODOLOGY AND ORGANIZATION OF THE STUDY

The present study is basically an empirical one. Relevant data for the study was collected from both primary and secondary sources. We adopted positional approach in identifying the sample for primary data collection. The sample size for the study constitutes of 221 respondents. As the location of habitation of the Galos spreads over about 18 administrative circles covering both East Siang and West Siang district excluding Upper Subansiri district[50], we included five administrative circles (two from East Siang and three from West Siang district) and three villages from each circle. Adequate care was also taken to represent both the hilly areas and the plain areas. Hence, two circles from foothill areas and three from the hilly areas were selected. The selection of the village was on the basis of location of the villages—a village nearest to the circle headquarter, one in between the border area of the circle and circle headquarter and the third one was from the village away from the circle headquarter of each circle. This was done to get more representative information of the different villages. While adopting the empirical survey method, primary data was collected from the sample, which constituted of both the traditional leaders as well as the modern leaders. For the purpose of this study, traditional leaders consisted of *Gaon Burah/Gam*, village elders (*Nyikok*) and the priest

50. The Galos are found in Dumpurijo and Baririjo circle of Upper Subansiri district also.

(*Nyijik*). The *Gaon Burah/Gam* meant the official *Gam* appointed by the district administration under the framework of the Assam Frontier (Administration of Justice) Regulation, 1945. The village elders are those leaders of the village who did not held formal position but instrumental in decision-making. The priest (*Nyijik/Nyibuh*) is the sacred leaders and considered as the custodian of the traditional belief system. Further, the modern leaders, in our study, consisted of the Panchayat leaders, party leaders and the church leaders. The Panchayat leaders consisted of Gram Panchayat Members and the Anchal Samity Members of the last Panchayat term. The party leaders consisted of those who hold a party office like president and secretary of any political party at village or the block level. Here, the church leaders do not necessarily mean the religious or Christian leaders. They have been grouped under the modern leaders because many of them were party office bearer or the Panchayat members. The data have been collected through the technique of person to interview with the help of suitably designed open-ended structured interview schedule. Data were also collected from the secondary sources as per the requirement of the chapters of the study from various sources. Informal discussion with certain leaders, both traditional and modern has been used at times of strengthen the arguments. Further, we adopted simple method of calculation to analyse the data. The fractions below .50 were ignored and above .50 were taken as 1. The percentages are given in the brackets.

For the purpose of our study, we interviewed 221 leaders. The respondent leaders were divided into two categories *viz.*, traditional leader and modern leader which was further sub-divided into different types of leaders namely GAM, Village Elders (VE) Priest (PR), Panchayat Member (PM), Party Leaders (PL) and Church Leader (CL). The letter "TL" stands for total and "G.TL" for grand total. Such abbreviation is being used in all the tables throughout the book. The category of traditional leaders constitutes of the *Gam*, Village Elder (VE), Priests (PR) and the modern leaders constitutes of Panchayat Members (PM), Party Leaders (PL) and Church Leaders (CL).

2

Profile of Arunachal Pradesh and the Galos

Arunachal Pradesh, the first land in India to greet the mother Sun (*Ane Donyi*)[1] , is home for about twenty five tribes and sub-tribes with total population of 10,96,702[2] including non-tribal population. The major tribes of Arunachal Pradesh are the Monpas, the Sherdukpens, the Akas, the Nishis, the Tagins, the Apatanis, the Hill Miris, the Adis, the Mishmis, the Khamptis, the Singphos, the Wanchos, the Noctes etc. Each tribe of Arunachal Pradesh has their own dialect with different socio-political traditions and the colourful festivals. They are said to speak a Tibeto-Burman group of language. The racial affiliation of the tribes of Arunachal Pradesh is described as Mongoloid, Paleo-Mongoloid and Proto-Mongoloid with considerable difference of opinion. To quote Choudhary, "the tribes of present Arunachal Pradesh with their variations of so-called Mongoloid character had a South-East Asian origin and their migration to their present area of dispersion took place from that direction in prehistoric times"[3] .

Arunachal Pradesh covers a large geographical area of about 83,743 sq. kms. and is bound by Assam in the south, Bhutan in the west, Tibet and China in the north and Burma

1. Many Tribal Groups in Arunachal consider *Donyi-Polo* (Sun-Moon) as God.
2. Provisional Census Report, 2001.
3. Choudhary, J.N., *Arunachal Pradesh from Frontier Tracts to Union Territory*, Cosmos Publication, 1983, p. 69.

in the east. With its rejuvenating streams and rivers and picturesque mountain hills, it is a natural home for many varieties of flora and fauna. The topography of Arunachal Pradesh consists of snow-clad mountains at higher altitude, beautiful valleys and plateaus, inaccessible terrains, dense tropical forest and occasional plains especially in the areas bordering Assam. The 24th state of Indian union, the modern Arunachal comprise of 16 administrative districts. It has sixty member Legislative Assembly and sends three representatives in the Union Parliament (two in the Lok Sabha and one in the Rajya Sabha). Corresponding with the development in other sphere, the state has numerous schools, seven colleges and one university. Once described as 'hidden land', now Arunachal has joined the national mainstream in every aspect.

Since the tribes of Arunachal Pradesh lack a script of their own, the Khampti being an exception, the people themselves have not preserved any recorded history because of which it becomes difficult to present a history of this land and its people. The written records about these tribes are started to get from the Ahom period when the tribals occasionally came down to the plains for salt and other items of necessary use. To quote Choudhary again, 'they were also known to indulge occasionally in depredations in the plain areas contiguous to the hills, and were sometimes involved in the clashes with the forces of Ahom ruler. At times, they were also known to serve in the Ahom army"[4] . The Ahom rulers pursued a policy of conciliation and isolation towards the hill tribes. The Ahoms introduced the policy of keeping the tribesmen living in the frontier in good humour and to do this, a form of *Posa* was evolved. The word '*Posa*' literally means a collection of subscription for a common purpose. Posa is defined in the official glossary of terms as allowances paid to certain hill tribes inhabiting the hills on the northern frontier of Assam..., on account of commuted blackmail or in consideration of the abandonment by them their claims with regards to certain *duars*. The tribals of the frontier hills

4. Chowdhary, J.N., *Arunachal Pradesh from Frontier Tracts to Union Territory*, Cosmos Publication, 1983, p. vii.

used to descend annually to the plains and levy blackmail from the border villages. The blackmail was levied in kind and it appears that the quantities demanded from each village or hamlet were fixed and well known to both parties; and as no individual inhabitant of a plains village was liable for any particular article, the whole amount was raised collectively by a village subscription or *Posa*. However, this term came to be applied to all payments made to hill tribes by the government, whether they were in communication of the blackmail or merely police payment under treaty obligation[5]. The right of *Posa* as claimed by the tribals were recognized or granted by the Ahom rulers.

After seeking British help to curve the Moamarian revolution (1792) by which the revolution was put to an end, the Ahom sought the British help for second time to drive out the Burmese occupation army. Consequently, the British forces defeated the Burmese army and the Treaty of Yandaboo was concluded in February 1826 AD, which ended the Burmese occupation of Assam, thereby paving the way for final annexation of the whole of Assam in 1838 AD. Thus, it is from the time of British rule over Assam that we get more detail history of these hill tribes from their tour diaries, records, reports and accounts. Though we do not have detail history of the region before the Ahom rule, the region was not unknown in the ancient times also. To quote Choudhary again, 'The Vedas and the Puranas, the epics like the Ramayana and the Mahabharata particularly, make specific reference to the region and the people of the mountainous terrain, ... the hill tribes of the Himalayan zone are the Kiratas mentioned in the ancient literature such as the Mahabharata, the Ramayana and the Puranas specially indicate their situation both in the north and east"[6]. Besides, the archaeological sites like Bhismaknagar of Lohit district, Malinithan of West Siang district, Itafort of present Itanagar, etc. are also a testimony that this region was

5. See L.N. Chakravarty *Glimpses of the Early History of Arunachal*, Directorate of Research, Govt. of Arunachal Pradesh, Itanagar, 1973, pp. 122-134.

6. Chowdhary, J.N., *Arunachal Pradesh from Frontier Tracts to Union Territory*, Cosmos Publication, 1983, p. ix.

inhabited in the dim past also. "But history furnishes a very imperfect insight into the origin and descent of the tribes of the North East Frontier. It seems almost vain to attempt to lift up the dark veil which conceals the origin of the tribes, to trace back their history, or to gain any information of the various revolutions by which they have been influenced; these subjects belongs to times and circumstances which are beyond the limit of certain knowledge. It would be the most cautious and perhaps the most philosophical course, to abstain from any conjecture relative to their origin or from any attempt to penetrate into the nature of causes of which even the most distant results are but partially known to us. Therefore, we must depend on the reflected light which is obtained by the comparison of language, by the analysis of civil and religious institutions and mythological fables, or by tracing marked affinities in the manners and customs of different tribes"[7].

The political evolution of Arunachal Pradesh starts from the Inner Regulation of 1843, a line fixed by the British government to guide the Civil Officer as to how far their jurisdiction extend and to contain the hill tribes within their territory, the purpose of which was basically to regulate the commercial relation between the hill tribes and the British subject in the plains. Once a part of Assam, the present Arunachal Pradesh was known as North East Frontier Tract as designated under the Assam Frontier Tract Regulation in 1914 AD. As such the North East Frontier Tract was divided into three administrative sections *viz.*, the Central and Eastern section with headquarter at Sadhiya, the Western section with headquarter at Charduar and the Lakhimpur Frontier Tract under the Deputy Commissioner of Lakhimpur district of Assam. These divisions were later re-designated as Sadhiya Frontier Tract, Balipara Frontier Tract and Lakhimpur Frontier Tract. Under the Government of India Act, 1919, all the tribal areas in Assam including North East Frontier Tract were designated, as 'Backward Area' and Dyarchy had no meaning for these Frontier Tracts.

7. Robinson (1841), as quoted in *History of Arunachal Pradesh* by M.L. Bose, Concept Publishing Company, New Delhi, 1997, p. 17.

Till 1943, these areas were loosely administered as 'Excluded Areas' as designated in Government of India Act, 1935 but in 1943 a change in the administrate set up was effected with the creation of new frontier tract known as Tirap Frontier Tract which was curved out of Sadhiya and Lakhimpur Frontier Tract with headquarter at Margerita. Inspite of too rapid punitive expeditions, the British were cautious enough not to disturb the functioning of the traditional political institutions of the tribals. But, the Assam Frontier (Administration of Justice) Regulation, 1945 was a clear indication of interference in the tribal system of crime and punishment, though for better improvement. The Regulation accepted the authority of the village councils, village headman and chieftaincy wherever they existed. The *Gaon Buras* or *Gam*, designated as village authority, were appointed and had to function within the framework of the Regulation though the Regulation did not explicitly use the expression '*Gaon Bura*'. Besides *Gaon Buras*, the Government appointed Political Interpreter and Political *Jamadar* also who were practically acting as an agent of the administration in the villages. In this way, the 'village democracy was weakened and the governmental control was extended'[8] to the tribal villages. After independence, the position of the North East Frontier Tract was hotly debated in the constituent Assembly, which ultimately led to the constitution of a committee popularly known as the Bordoloi Committee under the aegis of the Constituent Assembly to recommend special administrative framework for the tribal areas. But the committee did not favour any change in the existing administrative set up of the North East Frontier Tract. For more viable administration, the Balipara Frontier Tract was already divided into Sela sub-agency and the Subansiri area in 1946. Two years later, the Sadhiya Frontier Tract was also divided into the Abhor Hills and the Mishmi Hills with headquarter at Pasighat and Tezu respectively. The independent Indian government decided to push the administration further up to the Mac Mahan

8. Nyori, T., *History and Culture of the Adis*, Omsons Publications, 1993, p. 138.

Line which lead to the shifting of headquarter to further north. Thus, the position before 1954 were as follows :

(1) Sela Sub Agency with headquarter at Bomdila.

(2) Subansiri Area with headquarter at Lakhimpur.

(3) Abhor Hills with headquarter at Pasighat.

(4) Mishmi Hills with headquarter at Tezu.

(5) Tirap Frontier Tract with headquarter at Margherita.

The most remarkable change in the history of the North East Frontier Tract was the promulgation of the North East Frontier (Administration) Regulation of 1954, which inaugurated a full-scale administration of the area under collective designation of the North East Frontier Agency (NEFA), and erstwhile Frontier Tracts were re-designated as Frontier Division each under a Political Officer.

As a result, the whole NEFA was divided into six Frontier Divisions *viz.*, *(i)* Kameng Frontier Division, *(ii)* Subansiri Frontier Division, *(iii)* Siang Frontier Division, *(iv)* Lohit Frontier Division, *(v)* Tirap Frontier Division, *(vi)* Tuensang Frontier Division, which was transferred to Nagaland later on. By that time the rural reconstruction programme known as Community Development Programme was already extended to these frontier areas. For more effective frontier administration, a new cadre of the Indian Frontier Administrative Service (IAFS) was constituted which was, later on, absorbed into IAS cadre. The major administrative changes after the institution of NEFA was the constitution of Daying Ering Committee (1954) basically to explore and report on the feasibility of the introduction of modern democratic decentralization in the then NEFA. The recommendation of the Ering Committee became the basis for the enactment of the NEFA (Panchayati Raj) Regulation of 1967, which virtually ushered into the introduction of the three-tier Panchayati Raj system in NEFA. Further, as a result of the Ering Committee recommendation, the administration of NEFA was handed over to the Home Ministry of India from External Affairs Ministry. At the same time the nomenclature of the administrative division was changed to that of District such as Kameng District,

Subansiri District and so on. Correspondingly, the Political Officers, Assistant Political Officer, etc. were re-designated as Deputy Commissioner and Assistant Commissioner respectively. Thus, with the introduction of three-tier democratic decentralization under the framework of Ering Committee recommendation, the previous policy of isolationism ended and the NEFA was brought under the national mainstream.

The next important event in the political evolution of this frontier state was the enactment of the North-Eastern Areas (Reorganization) Act of 1971. The basic purpose of the Act was "to provide for the establishment of the states of Manipur and Tripura and to provide for the formation of the state of Meghalaya and of the Union Territories of Mizoram and Arunachal Pradesh by reorganizing the existing state of Assam and for matters connected therewith"[9] . So far the NEFA was concerned, the Act separated it from Assam and converted into a Union Territory to be called as Arunachal Pradesh. The existing Agency Council was also converted into Pradesh Council. The President of India appointed K.A.A. Raja as the first Chief Commissioner of Arunachal Pradesh in January 1972. The Act also provided for one seat each in the Lok Sabha and the Rajya Sabha from Arunachal Pradesh to be elected indirectly by the Electoral College. The Chief Commissioner was authorized to constitute a body of five Councellors, which acted as advisory and recommendatory body but later on, the Chief Commissioner transferred all the development departments to the control of the Councellors. The Pradesh Council and the body of Councellors started to function as defacto legislature and defacto cabinet respectively. The democratic process, which had begun to take place in Arunachal Pradesh by 1969, got gradual maturity with the introduction of the universal adult franchise for the first time in Arunachal Pradesh in 1972 for election to the Panchayat bodies. The process got further maturity with the conversion of the Pradesh Council into a Provincial Legislature and the body of Councellors into a

9. Singh, Chandrika as quoted in *Emergence of Arunachal Pradesh as a State*, Mittal Publication, Delhi, 1989, p. 129.

Council of Ministers. Mr. P.K. Thungon became the first Chief Minister of Arunachal Pradesh on August 13, 1975. But, the party politics was still new to the leaders of Arunachal Pradesh because no political parties took interest in the Arunachal politics though the Indian National Congress had already their unit established in 1972. The electoral politics started in Arunachal Pradesh with the flouting of the regional party known as the Peoples Party of Arunachal (PPA) in 1977 and since then, the Arunachal politics has witnessed a lot of defection and merger resulting in toppling of many ministries. Late Tomo Riba, the then Agriculture Minister, defected to the PPA because of which he was dropped from the Thungon ministry. The people of Arunachal Pradesh exercised their franchise for the first time in 1977 general election to elect their representative in the Lok Sabha. Shri R.K. Khirmey and late Bakin Pertin became the first elected representative of Arunachal Pradesh in the Lok Sabha[10]. After the Congress debacle in 1977 Parliamentary Election, Mr. Thungon, the Chief Minister of Arunachal Pradesh, along with his council of minister, defected to the Janata Party. The first Assembly Election in Arunachal was held in February 1978, which was keenly contested between the Janata Party and Peoples' Party of Arunachal (PPA). In this election, the Janata Party emerged victorious and hence, Thungon Ministry took the oath of office on 14th March, 1978. The Arunachal politics witnessed large-scale defection after the conclusion of the mid-term Assembly election of 1980 and ultimately, Shri Gegong Apang became the Chief Minister. Mr. Apang continued to serve as Chief Minster for 19 (nineteen) uninterrupted years and founded a new regional party known as Arunachal Congress (AC). But, the Apang Ministry was toppled in 1999 by his own party legislators and hence, the Indian National Congress (INC) under the leadership of Shri Mukut Mithi formed the government. 'Shri Gegong Apang, the lone A.C. legislator created history by dethroning the popularly elected congress government under the leadership of Mukut Mithi. An unprecedented political upheaval-

10. Pandey, B.B., *Arunachal Pradesh—Village State to Statehood*, Himalayan Publishers, Itanagar, 1997, pp. 188-190.

toppling of an elected government and formation of United Democratic Front (UDF) by the same legislators who later switch over to the Bharatiya Janata Party (BJP)—was the most eventful incident witnessed in this peaceful hill states in 2003'[11].

PROFILE OF GALOS

The Galos or (Gallong as they are known in the official parlance) is one of the major tribe of Arunachal Pradesh. Earlier known as Abhor, the Adi is used as blanket term for the entire tribe inhibiting the West Siang District, the East Siang district, the Upper Siang district, the eastern tip of Upper Subansiri district and western portion of Dibang Valley district. Thus, the Adis spread over five districts of Arunachal Pradesh. There are so many sub-tribes within Adis, the Galo being the major one. The other sub-tribes, which are included in the Adis, are the Minyongs, the Pasis, the Padams, the Milangs, the Pangis, the Karkos, the Simongs, the Ashings, the Tangams, the Boris, the Bokars, the Ramos and the Pailibos. Some writer has classified these tribes into two broad groups on the basis of the socio-linguistic affinity and genealogical similarity. Thus, they can be divided into two groups *viz.*, Galo group of the Adis and Minyong-Padam group of the Adis though there is no rigidity in such division rather it is only an academic interest. B.B. Pandey divided them as the Galoic group and the Padamic group[12]. Dr. Nyori divided them on the basis of the location of their habitation as eastern Adis and western Adis[13]. The Galos, Bori, Bokar, Pailibo and Ramo come under the Galo group and the rests under the Minyong-Padam group according to the above categorization. However, there is no parent tribe among the sub-tribes of the Adis by which a group may be named. Though Galo is one of the major sub-tribe of the Adis, they are different from other Adis in terms

11. "2003—A year that was for Arunachal", *Echo of Arunachal*, December 17, 2003, p. 1.

12. Pandey, B.B., *Leadership in a Tribal Society*, Spectrum Publication, Guwahati, 1991, p. i.

13. Nyori, T., *History and Culture of the Adis*, Omsons Publication, New Delhi, 1993, p. 4.

of dress, festivals, dialect, marriage, genealogy, hairstyle and social institutions, etc. "The social structure and institutions of the Gallongs are basically different from the other sections of the Adis"[14]. In this connection, Srivastava deserves to be quoted in considerable length. "But these authors (British authors) were not very precise in making a distinction between the Abors and the Gallongs. The Abor is a group of such people as the Minyongs, Padams, Panggis, Pasis and several others, while Gallong is another group of people differing from the Abor in dialect, customs—social and religious and mainly in hairstyle ...the Gallongs cannot be placed in the same group with the Abors"[15]. Indian Constitution also listed the Galo as separate tribe of Arunachal Pradesh apart from the Abors[16]. Many writers may confuse by two terms—Galo and Gallong. Actually, Gallong is a Minyong-Padam way of pronunciation because the later usually add 'ng' when a word ends in a vowel such as '*Ponung*' for '*Ponu*' and '*Kebang*' for '*Keba*'. Thus the earlier writers, especially the British used the word '*Gallong*' for Galo because of their earlier contact with the Minyong-Padam group of Adis.

HABITATION

The Galo settlements spread over entire West Siang district excepting few administrative circles like Minigong, Mechuka, Kaying, Payum, Rumgong and Tato where there is mixed settlement with the other Adis. Dumpurijo and Baririjo circle in eastern Upper Subansiri district and Nari, Koyu and Seren circles in south-west tip of East Siang district is also inhabited by the Galos. The Galo is surrounded by Bori and Bokar in the north, the Assam plains in the south, the Tagins and Hill Miris in the west and the Padam-Minyong group of Adis in the east. Their habitat is the great Himalayan slope, which extends up to the northern basins

14. *NEFA, the Land and the People*, Directorate of Information and Public Relation, NEFA Administration, Shillong, 1968, p. 14.
15. Srivastava, L.R.N., *The Gallongs*, Directorate of Research, Govt. of Arunachal Pradesh, Itanagar, 1962, p. 8.
16. Third Schedule, Part XVIII of Indian Constitution (Schedule Tribe Order, 1950).

of Brahmaputra, characterized by hilly terrain with occasional plains, valleys and gorges and beautiful plateaus where main settlements are concentrated.

The large evergreen forest in these lofty hill areas houses many types of animals. The tiger, panthers, elephants, deer, monkeys, squirrels, rats, pigeons, hornbills, wild pigs, snakes and various other reptiles are abundant here. Thick jungles with tall and stout trees, bushes, creepers, shrubs, bamboo, cane, etc. are the characteristics of this luxuriant evergreen vegetation. The prominent rivers in the Galo area are Sinyen, Dobu, Ego, Sigen, Hirik, Hiru, Yomgo and Sipu, besides these, many smaller rivers and streams criss-cross the hills to ultimately join with the bigger rivers and finally joins the mighty Brahmaputra in Assam. The Galo dialect conforms to the general characteristics of the other Adis, Nishis, Hill Miris and the Tagins. There are close linguistic affinities among these groups. But within Galo also there are number of sub-dialect, which are slightly different from one another. "The competent authorities, who have done work on the dialect of the NEFA, class Gallong in the North Assam group of the Tibeto-Burman language"[17].

It will be very interesting to note that all the Galo can trace their genealogical route of origin right from Abotani, the legendary ancestor, down to self. All the Galos believe themselves as the progeny of Abotani. Here, Abo means father and Tani literally means a man. Thus, Abotani can be inferred as the father of mankind according to the Galo mythology. Such genealogical memory is possible among the Galo only because of the peculiar system of naming of an individual. Being a patriarchal society, a Galo always prefix the second syllable of his father's name in his own name. Suppose, author's grandfather's name was Nyitu, so authors father's name is Ture and author's name is Rejir, then author's child's name will start from 'Jir' only. Thus, it goes like this—Nyitu—Ture—Rejir—Jirjum so on. "This is in way, similar to the system adopted by the International

17. Srivastava, L.R.N., *The Gallongs*, Directorate of Research, Govt. of Arunachal Pradesh, Itanagar, 1962, p. 7.

Union of Pure and Applied Chemistry for naming chemical compounds. Just as the children derive (part of) their genes from their father, the names of the children are derived from the father's. The system is reliable since deletion or inclusion of any name in the chain is considered inauspicious"[18]. Equivalent to Mr. And Ms., the prefix 'Ta' and 'Ya' is added in a name where no reference is made to the father. Male name starts with 'Ta' as 'Tare', 'Tajir' and female name starts with 'Ya' as 'Yapi', 'Yarik'. The Galos strongly believe in the sanctity of their genealogy. Every Galo is supposed to know his genealogical route of origin right from Abotani to himself otherwise; he may be looked down upon.

HISTORY

The early history of the Galo area is totally lies in a remote obscurity chiefly because of the absence of the indigenous script. It was a land unknown to the civilized world till the advent of the British. There is no archaeological site of importance in Galo area, excepting the Malinithan at foothill area bordering Assam in West Siang district, to justify or conjecture the existence of any human civilization. So, it is very much difficult to ascertain the beginning of the human habitation in these dark Himalayan terrains. But, the Galo being rich in oral history has their own version of history starting from the creation of the first mankind down to the present generation. But, within Galo also, there are many versions of origin and migration but all indicating the north. Hence, the Galos are believed to be the migrant from the northern side of their present habitation.

The British too has left no account of the Galo areas to construct a recent history. All the hitherto Abor-British relations were basically the British relationship with the Padam-Minyong groups of the Adis. Excepting some survey party and occasional tour, the British did not extend their regular administration in the Galo areas during the heydays of their power. Thus, Galo's relationship with the British

18. Karlo, T., *Nyoi Genealogical Map* (1st ed.), Nyoi Welfare Association, 1998, p. i.

was casual, occasional and very limited. To quote Srivastava again, "Whatever account is available—very scanty though—it is about the Abors. Earlier writers, who invariably entered through the Minyong Abor region, could not penetrate into the Galo areas and very little could be known about them"[19]. The Galos too did not organize any concerted effort to fight against the British or to defy the authority of the government.

The first instance of the conflict with the British occurred in 1848 when the Galos carried away ten gold-washers and the Beheah[20] headman to their hills to take revenge for stopping the conciliatory payment. The Adis used to claim absolute right over the gold and fish of Brahmaputra and other rivers coming down from their hills. To rescue the captives, the British sent an expedition under captain Vetch in February 1848. The expedition was sent against the Galos of the valley of Igo river,[21] and hence, the captives were rescued. The British activity in the Galo territory was mostly confined to the foothill areas only. There is no remarkable event occurred in Galo areas except occasional visits and punitive expeditions. In 1907, Noel Williamson paid a friendly visit to some Galo areas. Even during the well-known Abhor-war of 1911-12, the British troops destroyed some Galo villages, which lies to the west of Ledum. The Ledum column of the Abhor expedition under Lindsay marched up to Kakki destroying Kora and Dosi, which was suspected to be conniving with the Minyongs in the war. "The Galos poisoned the water with *Emo* (aconite) and *Tamo* (poison tree). This polluted water caused the column dysentery and many sepoys died"[22]. After the Abhor expedition, the British

19. Srivastava, L.R.N., *The Gallongs*, Directorate of Research, Govt. of Arunachal Pradesh, Itanagar, 1962, p. 8.
20. Nyori, T., *History and Culture of the Adis*, Omsons Publication, New Delhi, 1993, p. 98.
21. Nyori, T., *History and Culture of the Adis*, Omsons Publication, New Delhi, 1993, p. 98.
22. Osik, N.N., *British Relationship with the Adis*, Omsons Publication, New Delhi, p. 92.

extended their administered area further west up to Sinyen river and all the villages including the Galos which fall under the said area had to pay poll tax. By 1940's, the congress movement spread through the Galo areas. Some Galo leaders established a congress office and a primary school at Dipa. The movement was suppressed and leaders were arrested. The prominent congress activists during those days were Moje Riba, Moji Riba, Kore Bagra, etc.

SOCIETY

The Galo society largely conforms to the basic democratic norms. There is no social stratification as ruling class and subject class. Each and every one is considered as equal in the society. The Galo society is clearly reflected in the following words of Bhattacharjee, "Moving among the people, I was amazed to see a tension-free society. Here, casteism does not bar anybody nor there are clash between rich and poor. Here, community work is done by every one—an obligatory function of each individual and none can escape from the customary law. *Kebang* met justice on anyone found guilty rich or poor alike. While on work, all share the food from the same plate and sit together as equal partners. What is more striking is the self-reliance of the people—young and old. Begging is unknown as also the famine and pestilence"[23].

CLAN

As stated earlier, the Galos trace their origin from common ancestor—a human being, not from any object of nature or of the animal kingdom. Abotani is the common ancestor of the Galos and dispersion took place from him. The Galo society is divided into various clans who are the direct descendents of Abotani. The descent is always patrilineal. The following genealogical map illustrates the division of Galo society into clans.

23. Bhattacharjee, T.K., *Alluring Frontiers*, Omsons Publication, Guwahati, 1988, p. 108.

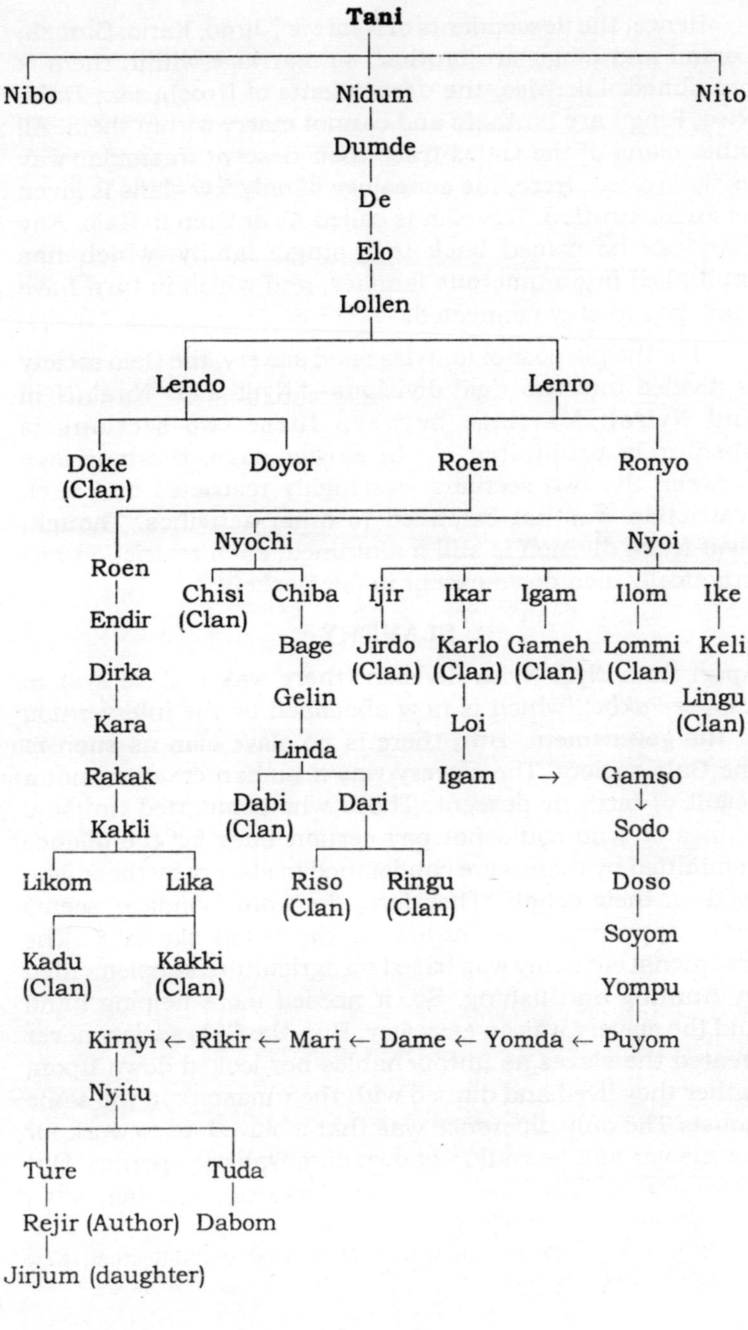
Tani
Nibo
Nidum
Nito
Dumde
De
Elo
Lollen
Lendo
Lenro
Doke (Clan)
Doyor
Roen
Ronyo
Nyochi
Nyoi
Roen
Chisi (Clan)
Chiba
Ijir
Ikar
Igam
Ilom
Ike
Endir
Bage
Jirdo (Clan)
Karlo (Clan)
Gameh (Clan)
Lommi (Clan)
Keli
Dirka
Gelin
Lingu (Clan)
Kara
Loi
Linda
Rakak
Igam → Gamso
Dabi (Clan)
Dari
Kakli
Sodo
Likom
Lika
Riso (Clan)
Ringu (Clan)
Doso
Soyom
Kadu (Clan)
Kakki (Clan)
Yompu
Kirnyi ← Rikir ← Mari ← Dame ← Yomda ← Puyom
Nyitu
Ture
Tuda
Rejir (Author)
Dabom
Jirjum (daughter)

Hence, the descendents of Nyoi *viz.*, Jirdo, Karlo, Gameh, Lommi and Lingu are brother, so marriage within them is prohibited. Likewise, the descendents of Nyochi *viz.*, Dabi, Riso, Ringu are brothers and cannot marry within them. All other clans of the Galos trace their descent in similar way as illustrated. Here, the genealogy of only few clans is given as an illustration. The clan is called Ali or Opin in Galo. Any clan can be traced back to a single family, which has multiplied into numerous families, and which in turn have managed to stay connected.

"For the purpose of marriage and slavery, the Galo society is divided into two rigid divisions—' Nyiji' and ' Nira' (Nyiji and Nyira). Marriage between these two sections is absolutely prohibited"[24]. In earlier days, the marriage between the two sections was highly restricted and such restriction was not extended to other activities. Though, Nyiji-Nyira division is still maintained, such restriction has practically died down except in few pockets.

SLAVERY

Apart from Nyiji-Nyira division, there was a slave system (*Pakne-Pakbo*), which is now abolished by the intervention of the government. But, there is no slave clan as such in the Galo society. The slavery was a human creation, not a result of birth or descent. Those who committed unusual crimes or who could not pay certain fines for the offence committed by them were condemned to slavery by those who paid on their behalf. 'Therefore, the word 'bondage' seems more appropriate in context of the tribal slaves'[25]. The traditional economy was based on agriculture supplemented by hunting and fishing. So, it needed more helping hand and the slavery was an easy way. But, the Galo society never treated the slaves as untouchables nor looked down upon, rather they lived and dinned with their masters in the same house. The only difference was that a slave had to work for his master and he could not own immovable properties. But

24. "*NEFA, the Land and the People*", Directorate of IPR, NEFA Administration, Shillong, 1968, p. 14.

25. Negi, D.S., *A Tryst with Mishmi Hills*, Tushar Publication, New Delhi, 1996, p. 96.

for the outsider, it was almost impossible to differentiate the master and slave in the village. There was complete social mingling. 'But the echo of deep-rooted stigma of the slavery is still to be heard in the Galo society'[26]. The marriage between the liberated slaves and non-slaves is very rare in these days also particularly in the rural areas.

WOMEN

Though the Galo society is a patriarchal society, the women are respected and treated as equal in the society. A woman becoming a *Gam* and priest (*Nyibuh*) is not unknown in the society. But women generally do not take part in the deliberations of the village council (*Keba*) and other corporate decision-making forum though their taking part is not a taboo. A close scrutiny reveals that the women has got separate role in the family and village affairs. She remains tied to the usual household activities of cooking, serving, washing, feeding the domestic animals, managing firewoods and so on. In short, she is the last to retire at night and the earliest to get up in the morning. In field, women's role is more important in sowing; weeding and reaping nevertheless both husband and wife accompany each other in all activities. The headship of the mother is not subordinate in a Galo family. However, in the village affairs, the women usually perform dances and songs (*Ponu-Nyitom*) for entertainment on occasions. They prepare '*Opo* or *Poko*' (local drinks), rice and serve them to the villagers. They also take part in some community work, but in such, their role is mainly of assistance.

MARRIAGE

The marriage system in the Galo society has undergone a considerable change under the impact of modernization and development. Many of the earlier systems have been completely discarded. In the traditional Galo society, there were basically three types of marriages—*(i)* normal marriage, *(ii)* child marriage and *(iii)* womb marriage (*Neppe Nyida*), a kind of advance marriage when a child is still in the mother's

26. Nyori, T., *History and Culture of the Adis*, Omsons Publication, New Delhi, 1993, pp. 211-215.

womb. The 'womb marriage', though not popular, was a peculiar type of marriage system. In such system, two families comes to an agreement before the birth of a child that after birth, if one's is a son, their marriage would be solemnized and, the process of 'give and take' starts henceforth as in the normal marriage. This system has been discarded. Both 'womb marriage' and the child marriage were used to take place between two traditional friends (*Keden*) to retain their friendship. Usually, Galo marriage is negotiated. The process of marriage starts with the moment the marriage proposal (*Nyida Tanam*) comes into being but the actual marriage differs according to the will of both the parties. The most popular marriage ceremony is the mithun sacrifice (*Togu*), which is performed in several stages. So, it is a lengthy process. But, the *Togu* is not a necessary or unavoidable part of the marriage ceremony. Most of the people get married without performing *Togu*. The marriage is considered to be consummated when '*Agam-Layap*' is finally performed. In *Agam-Layap*, small altar is made and a foul is sacrificed and the priest use to chant the related mythology. After *Agam-Layap* only, the couple is recognized by the society as legitimate husband and wife. The customary bride-price (*Are*) is usually two mithuns, and if any excess numbers of mithun are given, it has to be refunded by the girls' family in the form of *Adam-Tadok* (disc and beads) in rough proportion. It is an obligation, not compulsion, on the part of the groom to give meat and fish to bride's family at regular interval during his lifetime for which he will also get regular presentation in form of *Adam* and *Tadok*. After being married, a women's sexual relation with her husband's brothers of the same clan (*Sitem*) is not considered as incest or a taboos. But, it is neither an obligation nor the husband's brothers have absolute sexual right over her as many people may think so. Many writers termed this system as polyandrism but it is not polyandry in real sense of the term. B.B. Pandey termed the system as cicisbeism[27]. Such relationship depends on their

27. Sarkar, N.R., as quoted in *Leadership in a Tribal Society*, by B.B. Pandey, Spectrum Publication, Guwahati, 1991, p. 27.

intimacy and understanding of each other. But the system is dying fast especially in urban and semi-urban areas.

OCCUPATION

The main occupation of the Galos is agriculture both jhum and wet rice cultivation. In jhum cultivation, which is also called 'slush and burn' method of cultivation, several crops like paddy, maize, millet, chilli, beam, pumpkin, banana, sugarcane, etc. are grown. Off late people find it more reliable and assured production, to adopt wet rice cultivation. Nevertheless, the jhum is still very popular. Because of its multiple cropping pattern, there is lesser chance of crop failure in jhum and always serve as support in the lean period. Apart from agriculture, the main supplementary occupation are fishing, hunting, crafting and weaving.

RELIGION

The religious belief of the Galos is shrouded in numerous faiths and traditions, which are as old as the people themselves. The Galos believe in the existence of numerous deities (*Uyi* or *Uyu*) both benevolent and malevolent. The rites or rituals are performed to propitiate these deities. Though *Donyi-Polo* (Sun-Mood) is considered as supreme God and Galo conduct themselves in the name of *Donyi-Polo*, there is no organized prayer and established norms of worship to *Donyi-Polo* as other religions do have. All the rituals and sacrifices of animals are performed to appease different kinds of deities and spirits, which cause diseases or may bring prosperity. However, the new *Donyi-Poloism* is yet to enter into the Galo area. Like any other religion, the new *Donyo-Polo* religion has regular prayer centre and established methods of prayer, which is unknown to the traditional tribal faith. Besides indigenous faiths, many Galos have embraced Christianity.

3

Socio-Economic Background of the Leaders and Trends of Change

The socio-economic background of an individual, to a large extent, determines his early socialization, shapes his personality and influences his day-to-day interaction with other members of the community. Socio-economic background, in fact, places an individual in a specific position within his community and shapes his behavioural pattern in course of time. The values and personal convictions of a person are very much influenced by the environment to which he is exposed from the very beginning. Thus, the behaviour of the leaders is influenced, to a great extent, by the status accorded to them and the environment in which they grow and develop. The understanding of a man's early socio-economic environment is, therefore, essential for a proper understanding of his behaviour and actions. Such analysis can 'reveal leadership mobility indicative of general social mobility and discover the inflow of new social groups and leadership positions in a society'[1] especially when a society is in transition under the impact of the forces of modernization. The socio-economic status is defined as the position of an individual or a family occupied with reference to the prevailing average standards of cultural possession, effective income, material possession and participation in the group activities of the communities.[2] The socio-economic status of a leader may be both achieved

1. Singh, R.S. *Rural Elite, Entrepreneurship and Social Change*, Rawat Publication, Jaipur, 1985, p. 66.
2. As quoted by B.M. Verma in *Rural Leadership in a Welfare Society*, Mittal Publication, New Delhi, 1994, p. 60.

and ascriptive in nature. The changing socio-economic status of leaders may be adopted as index to the changing power structure.[3] The variables like sex, age, income, family size, education, landholding, property etc. are generally considered as an important factor in determining the leadership phenomenon in the rural and tradition-bound society like that of the Galos. This chapter tries to analyze the socio-economic background of the respondents (leaders) and study the trends of change in the leadership pattern in the Galo society.

SEX

The Galo society is patriarchal and patrilineal. The genealogical route is always traced through father and he is always the head of the family. But there is no marked social stigma attached to the status of women in Galo society. The absence of social stigma like dowry, *Sati* and *Purdah* make them comparatively safer in the family than their counterparts elsewhere in India. In household affairs, the women play a vital, if not leading role like the male member, however, in community affairs, the participation of women is negligible, if not nil. The leadership is not an exception. Following table 3.1 demonstrate the sex composition of leaders in the Galo society.

The table 3.1 reveals that out of 221 leaders, only 13 (thirteen) leaders *i.e.* 6 per cent are female and the rest 208 leaders *i.e.* 94 per cent are male. There are only 2 (two) women *Gam* who represent the traditional leadership. This table shows that the leadership in Galo society is predominantly a male affair. The reasons behind such negligible participation of women in the leadership process are the patriarchal structure of the society, subdued customary position of the women and women's sphere of activities being confined to household management. As the table reveals, sex is an important factor in leadership and hence, there is positive correlation between sex and leadership. Sex-wise breakup of the leaders reveals that

3. Choudhary, D.S., *Emerging Rural Leadership in an Indian State*, Manthan Publications, New Delhi, 1981, p. 44.

Table 3.1. Sex Composition of the Respondents

	Traditional leaders				*Modern leaders*				
Sex	*GAM*	*VE*	*PR*	*TL*	*PM*	*PL*	*CL*	*TL*	*G.TL*
Male	68 (97)	88 (100)	9 (100)	115 (98)	43 (93)	30 (100)	20 (71)	93 (89)	208 (94)
Female	2 (3)	N	N	2 (2)	3 (7)	N	8 (29)	11 (11)	13 (6)
Total	70 (100)	38 (100)	9 (100)	117 (100)	46 (100)	30 (100)	28 (100)	114 (100)	221 (100)

the emerging leadership has slightly greater number of women as compared to the traditional leaders. It is only 2 per cent among the traditional leaders but in case of the modern leaders, it is 11 per cent. The proportion of women is very low among the modern leaders too because this data was collected prior to the implementation of the 33 per cent reservation for women in the Panchayat bodies as per the Pachayati Raj Act, 1997.

AGE

Age is associated with experience and wisdom. "It has acquired a traditional importance in the society and considered to be an important factor in the Indian tradition of leadership. It symbolizes experience, maturity and equanimity of mind"[4]. "Age is a significant variable in the study of rural leadership because in the Indian village community, leadership has been the monopoly of the old persons who, in the past, dominated rural life in all its aspect"[5]. The same is the case with the leadership in various village councils in Arunachal Pradesh. In the traditional political structure of the Galos, the elders are accorded special status because they are well conversant with the customary codes and precedents coupled with sense of justice, responsibility and community feelings. Thus, leadership in decision-making process in the traditional council is basically that of the elders. But, the introduction of statutory panchayats and spread of party politics at the grassroot level has give definite impetus to the entry of younger people in the leadership structure. The analysis of leadership in relation to its age composition simply explains the mobility of younger generation into the leadership position[6]. Following table 3.2 shows the age composition of the leaders.

4. Verma, B.M., *Rural Leadership in a Welfare Society*, Manthan Publication, New Delhi, 1981, p. 61.
5. Choudhary, D.S., *Emerging Rural Leadership in an Indian State*, Manthan Publication, New Delhi, 1981, p. 45.
6. Singh, R.S., *Rural Elite, Entrepreneurship and Social Change*, Rawat Publication, Jaipur, 1985, p. 68.

Table 3.2. Age-wise Distribution of the Respondents

Age in years	*Traditional leaders*				*Modern leaders*				
	GAM	*VE*	*PR*	*TL*	*PM*	*PL*	*CL*	*TL*	*G.TL*
Below 30	N	N	N	N	6	2	3	11	11
					(13)	(7)	(11)	(11)	(5)
30 to 45	14	10	2	26	26	23	20	69	95
	(20)	(26)	(22)	(22)	(57)	(77)	(71)	(66)	(43)
46 to 60	30	20	3	53	12	4	4	20	73
	(43)	(53)	(33)	(45)	(26)	(13)	(44)	(19)	(33)
Above 60	26	8	4	38	2	1	1	4	42
	(37)	(21)	(44)	(32)	(4)	(3)	(4)	(4)	(19)
Total	70	38	9	117	46	30	28	104	221
	(100)	(100)	(100)	(100)	(100)	(100)	(100)	(100)	(100)

As above table shows, there is difference in age composition between the traditional leaders and the modern leaders. None of the respondents belonging to the traditional categories like *Gams*, village elders and priests are below 30 years whereas 11 per cent of the modern leaders are below the age of 30 years. The highest number of the respondents (45%) of the traditional leaders belong to the age group of 46 to 60 years, however, the highest proportion (66%) of the modern leaders belong to the age group of 30 to 45 years. Significantly, 32 per cent of the traditional leaders arc above the age of 60 years but it is only 4 per cent among the modern leaders. The leaders who were above the age of 60 years constituted 44 per cent of the priests followed by *Gams* (37%) and village elders (21%). As the table shows, relatively younger leaders are found among the panchayat members and the party leaders. The above analysis suggests that the modern leaders are younger in comparison to the traditional leaders. It also shows that there is a significant change in the traditional concept of rural leadership based on the age factor. Thus, age is no longer a criterion for the emerging leadership. It further reveals that a sort of shift is taking shape so far the age of the rural leadership is concerned is a resultant of the gradual decrease of the hold of the aged in the society.

FAMILY SIZE

The sociologists have defined family structure in terms of nuclear and joint family[7] . The joint family is larger in size. The Galos usually have joint family system. The members of the Galo joint families includes the grand parents, their children and grand children including the unmarried female members of the family. A big joint family has, sometimes more than one hearth or fireplace in a house and the total number of members may go up to 20-30 in a family. It is usually believed that a member of a large family has an advantage over others as he is assured of all-round support from his own family. Besides, in a larger family, some elder members usually get enough time for participation in the

7. Desai, A.R., *Rural Sociology in India*, Popular Prakashan, Bombay, 1969, pp. 31-32.

Table 3.3. Distribution of the Respondents Showing Their Family Size

Family size	Traditional leaders				Modern leaders				
	GAM	VE	PR	TL	PM	PL	CL	TL	G.TL
Below 5 members	6 (9)	4 (11)	2 (22)	12 (10)	7 (15)	2 (7)	5 (18)	14 (13)	26 (12)
6 to 10 members	33 (47)	21 (55)	4 (44)	58 (50)	27 (59)	13 (43)	20 (71)	60 (58)	118 (53)
11 to 15 members	17 (24)	11 (30)	1 (11)	29 (25)	9 (20)	8 (27)	2 (7)	19 (18)	48 (22)
Above 15 members	14 (20)	2 (5)	2 (22)	18 (15)	3 (7)	7 (23)	1 (4)	11 (11)	29 (13)
Total	70 (100)	38 (100)	9 (100)	117 (100)	46 (100)	30 (100)	28 (100)	104 (100)	221 (100)

village affairs. For the purpose of our study, we have divided the size of the family into 4(four) categories : *(i)* very small family *i.e.* below 5 members, *(ii)* small family *i.e.* 6-10 members, *(iii)* moderately large family *i.e.* 11-15 members and *(iv)* large family *i.e.* above 15 members. The following table 3.3 tries to focus on the correlation between leadership and the family size.

According to the table, majority (53%) of the leaders belong to the family size of 6 to 10 members. This is not a big family in Galo society where joint family happens to be the usual norm. It is followed by the leaders having the family size of 11 to 15 members (22%). The leaders having family size of above 15 members are only 13 per cent, which does not necessarily, reflects the relationship between family size and the leadership. The category-wise leadership pattern does not reveal any significant difference in relation to the family size. The leaders having very big family *i.e.* above 15 members constitute 15 per cent among the traditional leaders and 13 per cent among the modern leaders. The leaders from moderately big family *i.e.* 11 to 15 members constituted 25 per cent of the traditional leaders and 22 per cent of the modern leaders. The 50 per cent of the traditional and 58 per cent of the modern leaders were having family size of 6 to 10 members, and 10 per cent of the traditional leaders and 13 per cent of the modern leaders were having the family size of below 5 members. But, these differences in the proportion are too narrow to show a definite shift in the family size of the leaders. The present investigation reveals that the big family size does not have significant co-relation with leadership as it was thought. A member of a small family size can also be a leader, provided he establishes himself in the public estimation. As the table reveals, majority of the leaders are drawn from the smaller family size. This shift is an indication of the gradual split in the joint family norms. Therefore, it can be inferred that family size does not necessarily ensure leadership position and it is in no way a significant determinant in leadership formation rather it works in conjunction with other factors.

EDUCATION

Education is considered as a very important index of

Table 3.4. Distribution of the Respondents Showing Their Educational Background

Education	*Traditional leaders*				*Modern leaders*				*G.TL*
	GAM	*VE*	*PR*	*TL*	*PM*	*PL*	*CL*	*TL*	
Literate	24	24	N	48	34	25	24	83	131
	(34)	(63)		(41)	(74)	(83)	(86)	(80)	(59)
Illiterate	46	14	9	69	12	5	4	21	9
	(66)	(37)	(100)	(59)	(26)	(17)	(14)	(20)	(41)
Total	70	38	9	117	46	30	28	104	221
	(100)	(100)	(100)	(100)	(100)	(100)	(100)	(100)	(100)

modernization. It is also a very significant variable in the leadership analysis. Educated person is likely to be more adaptive to the changing socio-economic environment and understand the process of new institutions better. In the eye of the villagers, the educated persons are accorded certain degree of status and admiration as they have better contact with the outside world. They are expected to have better knowledge about official procedures, rules and regulations. In the traditional Galo society, education was not a criterion of leadership as there was no school in the Galo area prior to the independence. Since, all the people of the village were illiterate; the question of education as a determinant of leadership did not arise then. But the introduction of government schools and colleges have paved the way for mobility of more educated people in the leadership role. The following table 3.4 demonstrates the educational background of the leaders or role of education in the leadership trend.

The above table reveals that 59 per cent of the leaders are literate. For the purpose of our study, a person who simply can write and sign his name was considered as literate, that is why, the literacy percentage is significantly high. The modern leaders like the Panchayat members, the party leaders and the church leaders have higher percentage of literate 74 per cent, 83 per cent and 86 per cent respectively, whereas, the traditional leaders like *Gam*, village elders and the priests categories have comparatively lower percentage of literate—34 per cent, 24 per cent and 0 per cent respectively. The comparative study of the educational background of the leaders reveals that the total literacy percentage is higher among the modern leaders (80%) than the traditional leaders (41%). To make the picture clear, following table 3.5 shows the educational attainment of the leaders.

Though the literacy percentage is seemingly high, majority (43%) of them studied up to primary school which is followed by secondary level (24%), M.E. level (23%), college level (8%) and university level (2%) only. The level of educational attainment is comparatively higher among the

Table 3.5. Distribution of the Respondents Showing the Level of Their Educational Attainment

	Traditional leaders				*Modern leaders*				
Educational Attainment	*GAM*	*VE*	*PR*	*TL*	*PM*	*PL*	*CL*	*TL*	*G.TL*
Primary	19 (79)	6 (25)	N	25 (52)	12 (35)	5 (20)	14 (58)	31 (37)	56 (43)
M.E.	4 (7)	6 (25)	N	10 (21)	10 (29)	8 (32)	2 (8)	20 (24)	30 (23)
Sec.	1 (4)	9 (38)	N	10 (21)	6 (18)	8 (32)	8 (33)	22 (27)	32 (24)
College	N	2 (8)	N	2 (4)	6 (18)	3 (12)	N	9 (11)	11 (8)
Univ.	N	1 (4)	N	1(2)	N	1 (4)	N	1 (1)	2 (2)
Professional Course	N	N	N	N	N	N	N	N	N
Total	24 (100)	24 (100)	N	48 (100)	34 (100)	25 (100)	24 (100)	83 (100)	131 (100)

Note : This table reflects the response of the literate leaders only.

modern leaders. The leader who studied up to primary level only constituted 52 per cent of the traditional leaders and 37 per cent of the modern leaders but leaders who studied above the primary level was proportionately higher among the modern leaders—the leaders who read up to M.E. level constituted of 21per cent among the traditional leaders and 24 per cent among the modern leaders. Those who studied up to secondary level constituted 21 per cent of traditional leaders and 27 per cent of the modern leaders. Significantly, 79 per cent of the literate *Gam* studied up to primary level only followed by M.E. level (7%) and secondary level (4%). But the modern leaders like Panchayat members and party leaders have greater proportion (18% and 32%) respectively who read up to the secondary level. 18 per cent of the Panchayat members and 12 per cent of the party leaders studied up to the college level. One important trend that can be drawn is that considerably high proportion of the village elders studied up to the middle and secondary school level (25% and 38% respectively). This may seem strange to some extent but during the course of our interview, it was found that many of the village elders were unemployed literate. These 'young' elders are accorded a leadership status in the public estimation chiefly due to two reasons. Firstly, they are gifted with good knowledge about the tradition and precedents coupled with good oratorical skill. Secondly, they have definite advantage over others due to their formal educational background. They have better outlook and contact with the outside agency. Many of them were found to be having good rapport with the government officers and even the ministers. Thus, table 1.4 and 1.5 shows that though education was not a basic criterion of leadership in the traditional perspective but it is one of the most important determinants of the leadership in the emerging trends. Hence, there is a positive co-relationship between educational background and the emerging trends of leadership. Such shift may be attributed to the fact that the customary knowledge is not always relevant in the emerging leadership situation. Rather, people tend to prefer dynamism in the leadership role, which is better fulfilled by the literate leaders.

OCCUPATION

The economic status of a person plays a crucial role in leadership formation. "Economic status had been traditionally an important determinant of rural leadership in the past ..., the rich had always enjoyed greater authority over the rural masses"[8] . The village people usually try to maintain good relationship with the rich people so that he is assured of help during the time of crisis and disease. That is why; rich people command certain legitimacy over certain household whom he had helped materially or financially. The innocent people who get help from such rich man feel obliged and this obligation led to obedience and obedience ultimately lead to 'leading-following' relationship. Besides this, the rich people can donate money or material in public occasions like VIP visit, festivals, social gathering and community picnic. Such ready generosities on public occasions earn them admiration in the public opinion. Thus, it is usually consider that 'power and wealth usually go together'[9] . To ascertain the economic status of the leaders, variables like occupation, annual income, source of income, property, land holding, type of dwelling house etc. were analyzed. In addition to these variables, some specific questions were asked to the respondent (leaders) regarding the grand marriage celebration *(Togu)*, private feast offered to the public *(Hurin-Namrin)*, ready generosity on public occasions etc.

The shifting cultivation was the mainstay of the traditional Galo economy but, off late, the Galos have adopted the permanent wet rice cultivation in large scale. Thus, agriculture continues to be the main occupation of the Galos. The table 3.6 shows the occupational structure of the leaders.

The table 3.6 reveals that 90 per cent of the leaders are engaged in agriculture. It remains the main occupation of the leaders. Due to the opening up of new avenues of earning, some leaders have adopted allied occupation like

8. Dharshankar, *Leadership in Panchayat Raj*, Panchsheel Prakashan, Jaipur, 1979, pp. 89-90.

9. *Ibid.*, p. 90.

Table 3.6. Distribution of Respondents According to Their Occupation

Occupation	*Traditional leaders*				*Modern leaders*				
	GAM	*VE*	*PR*	*TL*	*PM*	*PL*	*CL*	*TL*	*G.TL*
Agriculture	68 (97)	32 (84)	9 (100)	109 (93)	42 (91)	23 (77)	25 (89)	90 (87)	199 (90)
Govt. contract	3 (4)	5 (13)	N	8 (9)	4 (9)	3 (10)	2 (7)	9 (9)	17 (8)
Private business	3 (4)	1 (3)	N	4 (3)	5 (19)	4 (13)	1 (4)	10 (10)	14 (6)

Note : Total number of respondent is not shown in the table as same respondents were engaged in more than one occupation. So, total exceeds the actual number of respondents.

government contract (8%) and private business (6%), but this does not show any major shift in general occupational structure of the leaders in the Galo society. But the comparative study of the occupation shows that comparatively larger proportions of the modern leaders are in some other occupation along with the agriculture. The proportion of leaders whose main occupation was only agriculture were 93 per cent among the traditional leaders and 89 per cent among the modern leaders, and those who engaged in government contract were 9 per cent each, but, the leaders who were engaged in the private business were only 3 per cent among the traditional leaders and 10 per cent among the modern leaders. 97 per cent of *Gam* and 100 per cent of the priests are agriculturist while it is comparatively lesser in case of modern leaders like Panchayat members (91%) and party leaders (77%). The proportions of agriculturist among village elders are comparatively low (84%) in comparison to the *Gam* (97%) due to the fact that the village elders, to some extent, represent both the old and new leadership. The data of this particular table shows that occupation is not a significant factor in overall leadership formation but in the emerging trends of leadership pattern, it has some significance.

INCOME

Income was the second factor in our study to determine the economic status of the leaders. Many studies have indicated that there is positive relationship between income and leadership. It is also widely believed that wealth is a basic criterion for leadership[10]. For the purpose of our study, the respondents were asked about their annual income in rupees. Since most of the leaders did not have permanent source of income, it was not feasible to determine their exact annual income. That is why, their income was categorized into ranges *viz.*, low income group (below Rs.10,000), moderate income group (Rs.10,000 to 25,000), high income group (Rs.26,000 to Rs.50,000) and very high income group (above Rs.50,000). The income mentioned over here is on

10. Choudhary, D.S., *Emerging Rural Leadership in An Indian State*, Manthan Publication, New Delhi, 1981, p. 54.

Table 3.7. Distribution of the Respondents as per Their Annual Income

	Traditional leaders				*Modern leaders*				
Income in Rs.	*GAM*	*VE*	*PR*	*TL*	*PM*	*PL*	*CL*	*TL*	*G.TL*
Below 10,000	42 (60)	18 (47)	4 (44)	64 (55)	17 (37)	16 (53)	16 (57)	49 (47)	113 (51)
10,000 to 25,000	24 (34)	12 (32)	3 (33)	34 (33)	22 (48)	7 (23)	10 (36)	39 (38)	78 (35)
26,000 to 50,000	N	2 (5)	N	5 (4)	2 (4)	6 (20)	1 (4)	9 (9)	14 (16)
Above 50,000	N	2 (5)	N	2 (2)	2 (4)	N	1 (4)	3 (3)	5 (2)
Can't determine	4 (6)	1 (3)	2 (22)	7 (6)	3 (7)	1 (3)	N	4 (4)	11 (5)
Total	70 (100)	38 (100)	9 (100)	117 (100)	46 (100)	30 (100)	28 (100)	104 (100)	221 (99)

the basis of the revelations made by the leaders themselves. Further the amount is drawn through approximation. Following table 3.7 shows the annual income of the leaders in terms of rupees.

The table reveals that majority (51%) of the leaders belongs to the low-income group, followed by moderate-income group (35%), high-income group (6%) and very high-income group (2%). However, 5 per cent of the leaders said that they could not determine their income in rupees. Thus, this study shows that income has limited role in the general leadership formation. The comparative analysis of the income of the leaders reveals a slight difference in the income level between the traditional and the modern leaders. The low-income group constituted 55 per cent of the traditional leaders but 47 per cent of the modern leaders. The 33 per cent of the traditional leaders had moderate income, but in case of the modern leaders, it was 38 per cent. The high-income group constituted 4 per cent of the traditional leaders and (9% of the modern leaders. The leader-wise breakup of the leaders' income demonstrate that none of the traditional leaders like *Gam* and priest belongs to the high income group, but 4 per cent of the panchayat members and 20 per cent of the party leaders belong to the high income group. Here, village elder is an exception due to the reasons explained earlier. Thus, this study shows that the emerging leadership is slightly better up in term of monetary income than the *Gams* and the priest. The reasons for this may be that proportionately higher numbers of emerging leaders are engaged in allied occupations like government contract and/or private business.

SOURCE OF INCOME

Though agriculture remains to be the main source of income in any traditional society, it is more so in a tribal society, the emerging scenario paves the way for other source of income like government contract works and trading or mortgaging trading licences. The major government contract works available in the rural areas includes road cutting, canal digging, electrical wiring and so on under the respective government departments. Further, the

Table 3.8. Distribution of the Respondents According to Their Source of Income

Income sources	Traditional leaders				Modern leaders				G.TL
	GAM	VE	PR	TL	PM	PL	CL	TL	
Agriculture	67 (96)	34 (89)	8 (89)	109 (93)	40 (87)	22 (73)	23 (82)	85 (82)	194 (88)
Govt. contract	3 (4)	4 (11)	1 (11)	8 (7)	8 (17)	4 (13)	2 (7)	14 (13)	22 (10)
Trading/ Mortgaging	1 (1)	3 (8)	N	4 (3)	6 (13)	1 (3)	1 (4)	8 (8)	12 (5)
Other	3 (4)	1 (3)	N	4 (3)	N	3 (10)	2 (7)	5 (5)	9 (4)

Note : Total is not shown as certain categories of leaders exceeds the total number of the respondents as some of them indicated more than one source of income.

government restricts the issue of trading licence to the non-tribals in Arunachal Pradesh. So, most of the tribals, who hold a trading licence, sublet their licence to the non-tribal businessmen. In this way, they get substantial recurring income. The supply and sell of wood and cane are other popular business in the rural areas. Table 3.8 shows the source of income of the leaders in Galo society.

The table reveals that agriculture is the main source of income. Income source of 88 per cent of the leaders was agriculture. The source of income like government contract and private business constitute 10 per cent and 5 per cent respectively. The leader-wise break-up of income source reveals that 96 per cent of *Gam's* source of income was agriculture followed by village elders and priest (89% each). But in case of Panchayat leader and party leader, it was marginally low *i.e.* 87 per cent and 73 per cent respectively. But in government contract, the percentage of modern leaders is higher than that of the traditional leaders. 17% of Panchayat members and 13 per cent of party leaders have government contract as source of income but it is slightly lower in case of *Gam* and the village elder *i.e.* (4%) and (11%) respectively. 9 per cent of total respondents had other source of income too, which includes occasional income from selling of poultry, cattle, properties like beads and bowls *(Adam-Tadok)* etc. The table further shows that 13 per cent of the panchayat leaders have earning from private business like trading and mortgaging the trading licence. 3 per cent of the party leaders and 4 per cent of the church leader have also similar source of earning. But, it is 1 per cent among *Gam* and no priest has such source of earning. Village elders' income through government contract and private business (11% and 8% respectively) is comparatively higher than the *Gam* and the priest due to the reasons explain earlier. The comparative analysis of the income source reveals that lesser proportion of the modern leaders are dependent on agriculture for their income than that of the traditional leaders. The proportion of leaders whose source of income was agriculture was 93 per cent among the traditional leaders but 82 per cent among the modern leaders whereas, the leaders who earn from government contract works was

7 per cent among the traditional leaders and 13 per cent among the modern leaders and those whose income was trading or mortgaging the trading licence was 3 per cent among the traditional leaders and 8 per cent among the modern leaders. The overall analysis of the table reveals that though agriculture remains the main source of income, the emerging leaders have wider source of income, which includes government contract works and private business such as trading and subletting the trading licence. Hence, agriculture, despite being the mainstay of the source of income, there is gradual shift in the same, which is reflected in the source of income of the modern leaders.

PROPERTY

Economic status of a person is assessed not by income alone but other indicators of wealth like property and land holding as well is equally important. Such indicator of economic status has greater relevance in the traditional economy where the income in term of rupees is negligible as well as difficult to ascertain. It was observed during the course of interview that considerable numbers of respondents were hesitant to disclose the income and tended to conceal the exact income. The possession of assets like gun, rice mill, vehicle, power tiller, *Adam-Tadok* etc. definitely symbolizes the economic status of a leader. Thus, income alone cannot determine the economic status. It may lack accuracy and reliability for meaningful conclusion. The following table 3.9 reveals the assets or movable property owned by the leaders.

The table 3.9 reveals that 10% of the leaders have vehicle. As regard to our study, vehicle includes both the four wheelers and two wheelers. Certainly, these leaders have high economic status in the rural society. Gun is usually considered as status symbol in traditional Galo society. Almost every household in the village aspires to own a gun. The table reveals that 46 per cent of the leaders have gun. Rice-mill is another important asset. The respondents having rice-mill are 26 per cent. Power tiller is limited *i.e.* 2 per cent only. Beads, bowls and disc (*Adam-Tadak*) is the traditional property of the Galos which is inherited from generation to generation. Almost every Galo

Table 3.9. Distribution of the Respondents Showing Their Property Ownership

	Traditional leaders				*Modern leaders*				
Properties	*GAM*	*VE*	*PR*	*TL*	*PM*	*PL*	*CL*	*TL*	*G.TL*
Vehicle	2 (3)	3 (8)	N	5 (4)	9 (20)	8 (27)	N	17 (16)	22 (10)
Gun	46 (66)	12 (32)	3 (33)	61 (52)	15 (33)	16 (53)	10 (36)	41 (39)	102 (46)
Rice mill	24 (34)	2 (5)	1 (11)	27 (23)	15 (33)	11 (37)	5 (18)	31 (30)	58 (26)
Power tiller	N	1 (3)	N	1 (1)	2 (4)	1 (3)	N	5 (5)	4 (2)
Adam-Tadok	67 (96)	21 (55)	7 (78)	95 (81)	35 (76)	24 (80)	24 (86)	83 (80)	178 (81)
Won't disclose	3 (4)	8 (21)	2 (22)	13 (11)	9 (20)	4 (13)	4 (14)	17 (16)	30 (14)

Note : The total is not shown, as many respondents possessed more than one type of property. So, total exceeds actual number of respondents.

household or couple possess *Adam-Tadok* jointly within the family or separately by couples. Some of these properties are inherited and some are earned through purchasing or presentation from wife's family. *Adam* means traditional bowls and disc of various categories. '*Tadok*' means beads or traditional necklace of different varieties. The *Adam-Tadok* has got greater antique value than the market value. They are used as medium of exchange, means of payment of compensation and fines etc within the Galo society. Though other tribes have also *Adam-Tadok*, there is relative difference of value. A certain type of costly *Adam* in Galo society may not necessarily be costly, for example, in the Nyishi society. In Galo society, the monetary value of *Adam-Tadok* ranges from few hundreds to lakhs. 81 per cent of the leaders, excluding those who preferred not to disclose, possess *Adam-Tadok*. As the respondents were not insisted to reveal their property in case of any hesitation, 14 per cent of them preferred not to disclose. This was done to remove the hesitation on other queries and earn their goodwill for frank discussion. The comparative study reveals that the higher proportion of the modern leaders owned modern assets like vehicle, rice-mill and power–tiller than the traditional leaders. The vehicle owner was 4 per cent among the traditional leaders but 16 per cent among the modern leaders. Those who own rice-mill were 23 per cent among the traditional leaders but 30 per cent among the modern leaders. The owner of the power tiller was 1 per cent among the traditional leaders and 5 per cent among the modern leaders. But the proportion of the leaders who owned traditional assets like gun and *Adam-Tadok* was slightly higher among the traditional leaders. Those who owned gun was 52 per cent among the traditional leaders and 39 per cent among the modern leaders, and the *Adam-Tadok* owner was 81 per cent and 80 per cent respectively. The gun is here considered as traditional assets because the licence for purchasing of gun was issued during the British administration also. The leader-wise breakup of the table reveals that only 3 per cent of *Gam* and 8 per cent of village elders own a vehicle but incase of panchayat leader and party leader, the vehicle owner is 20 per cent and 27 per cent respectively. The highest proportion of gun owner is *Gam* (66%) and highest proportion of *Adam-Tadok* owner is also *Gam* (96%). No *Gam* or priest owns a power tiller but in case of panchayat leader and party leader, its proportion is 4 per cent and 3 per cent respectively. Rice-mill owner among *Gam* is 34 per cent, village elder : 5 per cent and priest : 11 per cent only, but it is 33 per cent among panchayat members, 37 per cent among party leaders and 18 per cent among the church leaders. Thus, the table reveals that there is a shift in the nature of accumulation of property among the leaders. Comparatively, greater proportion of the emerging leaders own modern assets like vehicle, rice-mill and power tiller than the traditional leaders. Thus, in terms of assets, the leaders have good economic status. So, economic status is a significant factor in leadership formation.

MODE OF ACQUISITION OF PROPERTIES

The analysis of the mode of acquisition revealed that 30 per cent of the gun was inherited from their fathers. The respondent who inherited rice-mill was only 7 per cent, the rest were acquired. No vehicle and power-tiller were found to be inherited. But in case of *Adam-Tadok*, it was both acquired and inherited. The leader-wise break-up of the mode of acquisition revealed that the *Gam* who inherited gun was only 17 per cent but it was as high as 53 per cent among panchayat member and 44 per cent among party leaders. No *Gam* was found to have inherited rice-mill, but proportion of leaders who inherited rice-mill was 13 per cent among panchayat members and 18 per cent among the party leaders. Thus, this analysis reveals that the substantial proportion of the assets of new leaders are inherited which reveals some ascriptive factors in the property ownership but most of the leaders from the traditional category have acquired assets.

LAND

Land is considered as an important aspect of property in the traditional societies. "Land ownership was a crucial factor

11. As quoted in "Leadership in Panchayati Raj", by A.Y. Dharshankar, Panchsheel Prakashan, Jaipur, 1979, p. 90.

in establishing dominance in the village"[11]. It has special relevance in the context of traditional agrarian economy of the Galos. "Land ownership is often considered to be the most important source of power and prestige in rural Indian community"[12]. The agricultural land in Galo society may be broadly divided into two- jhumland and wetfield land. The Galos have the system of communal ownership of land; the forestland belongs the community, which is shared among the sub-clans going down to the level of family. In case of encroachment by any other villages, its defence is a collective responsibility, though particular patch of land is owned by a particular family. But, there is no formal landholding system and the system of measurement of the forestland. The boundaries of the forestland of the different family groups are marked by streams, rocks, big trees and the other natural topographical features. Since there is no specific transaction rate of the forestland, the rate is decided according to the wishes of both the seller and the buyer. However, this type of transaction is very rare. Except new migrants, which are very rare, every household in the village owns land individually or collectively. But the wet field land is a purely individual possession and the people do have the idea of measurement. Here, the wet field land means irrigated field where paddy is being usually cultivated. Horticulture is also a trend in the Galo society. Few leaders have commercial plots in the urban and semi-urban areas as well which is rented out. Table 3.10 shows the landholding of the leaders.

According to the table 3.10, 85 per cent of the leaders have jhumland at their disposal and the rest do not have jhumland because, few of them were new migrants and some of them were young leaders who were yet to inherit father's property. Alarmingly, 79 per cent of the respondents have wet rice field. Besides, 18 per cent of the leaders have horticultural garden and 3 per cent of them have commercial plots, which testify a shift in the traditional land use pattern. The comparison of the land possession reveals that 87 per cent of the traditional leaders and 83 per cent of the modern

12. Choudhary, D.S., *Emerging Rural Leadership in An Indian State*, Manthan Publication, New Delhi, 1981, p. 56.

Table 3.10. Distribution of the Respondents According to Their Landholding

Type of land	*Traditional leaders*				*Modern leaders*				
	GAM	*VE*	*PR*	*TL*	*PM*	*PL*	*CL*	*TL*	*G.TL*
Jhum land	60 (86)	33 (87)	9 (100)	102 (87)	37 (80)	25 (83)	24 (86)	86 (83)	188 (85)
Wetfield land	58 (83)	25 (66)	6 (67)	89 (76)	40 (87)	25 (83)	21 (75)	86 (83)	175 (79)
Horticulture garden	16 (23)	7 (18)	3 (33)	26 (22)	4 (9)	7 (23)	3 (11)	14 (13)	40 (18)
Commercial plots	5 (7)	N	N	5 (4)	N	1 (3)	1 (4)	2 (2)	7 (3)

Note : The total is now shown because respondents exceed the actual number of respondents, as many of them possessed more than one type of land.

leaders have the jhumland. The percentage of the leaders who possess wetfield land was 86 per cent among the traditional leaders and 83 per cent among the modern leaders. 22 per cent of the traditional leaders and 13 per cent of the modern leaders have horticultural garden, and those who have commercial plots constituted 4 per cent of the traditional leaders and 2 per cent of the modern leaders. The general impression of this analysis is that though the leaders have sufficient land possession, the difference in percentage among the different types of leaders was marginally low and hence, does not lead to any significant shift in the land possession for meaningful generalization. Nevertheless, it shows the fundamental aspect of property ownership which works as an important dimension of the over all pattern of leadership in Galo society.

SIZE OF LAND HOLDING (WET FIELD)

Since, most of the villages are located in the hilly areas, the scope for wet rice cultivation in large scale is very limited. Thus, considering the geographical constraints of the areas of our study, owning of approximately two or three acres of cultivable land is considered as an average possession. Further, due to the absence of the modern system of measurement of land, it is difficult to give the exact size of the wet field land. Taking this limitation into account, the size of the land is categorized as *(i)* average *i.e.* below 5 acres, *(ii)* high *i.e.* 5-10 acres and *(iii)* very high *i.e.* above 10 acres. Table 3.11 shows the land holding pattern of the wet field land of the leaders.

The table reveals that 45 per cent of the leaders have below 5 acres of land, which is considered as an average possession. 41 per cent have 5 to 10 acres and 14 per cent of them have very high possession *i.e.* above 10 acres. This study further confirms the higher status of the leaders in terms of land possession. The comparison of the size of land between the traditional and modern leaders reveals that the proportion of the leaders whose land was below 5 acres were 46 per cent and 44 per cent respectively, those having 5-10 acres were 40 per cent among the traditional leaders and 42 per cent among the modern leaders. And those having

Table 3.11. Distribution of the Respondents According to the Size of Their Land

Approx. size in acres	*Traditional leaders*				*Modern leaders*				
	GAM	*VE*	*PR*	*TL*	*PM*	*PL*	*CL*	*TL*	*G.TL*
Below 5	24	13	4	41	20	7	11	38	79
	(41)	(52)	(67)	(46)	(50)	(28)	(52)	(44)	(45)
5 to 10	28	7	1	36	14	13	9	36	72
	(48)	(28)	(17)	(40)	(35)	(52)	(43)	(42)	(41)
Above 10	6	5	1	12	6	5	1	12	24
	(10)	(20)	(17)	(14)	(15)	(20)	(5)	(14)	(14)
Total	58	25	6	89	40	25	21	86	175
	(100)	(100)	(100)	(100)	(100)	(100)	(100)	(100)	(100)

Note : The table reflects the response of 175 leaders who possess wet field land.

Table 3.12. Distribution of the Respondents Showing the Mode of Cultivation

	Traditional leaders				*Modern leaders*				
Mode of cultivation	*GAM*	*VE*	*PR*	*TL*	*PM*	*PL*	*CL*	*TL*	*G.TL*
Engage paid labour	43 (74)	15 (60)	2 (33)	60 (67)	28 (70)	22 (88)	17 (81)	67 (78)	127 (73)
Take help of clan member	5 (9)	4 (16)	1 (17)	10 (11)	5 (12.5)	1 (4)	N	6 (7)	16 (9)
Self	10 (17)	6 (24)	3 (50)	19 (21)	17 (17.5)	2 (8)	4 (19)	23 (27)	32 (18)

Note : (1) This table reflects the response of 175 leaders who own wet field land.

(2) Total is not given as certain category of respondents indicates more than one method of cultivation.

above the ten acres of wet field land were 13 per cent among the traditional leaders and 14 per cent among the modern leaders. Thus, the comparative study of the size of land between traditional and modern leaders does not reveal any significant pattern for meaningful study.

MODE OF CULTIVATION OF WET FIELD LAND

It is assumed that analysis of the mode of cultivation of wet field land would validate the size of the land because, to plough or cultivate large sized land, it needs more manpower. But, for smaller size land, the owners can do it by themselves. The following table 3.12 reveals the mode of cultivation of the wet field land by leaders.

The table reveals that 73 per cent of the leaders hire paid labourers to cultivate their land which indicates that most of the leader posses big size land which again have important relationship with their status. Hence, earlier generalization under table 1.11 is validated. 9 per cent of the leaders take the help of clan members to cultivate their land, which also suggest that size of their land is above average. Only 18 per cent confessed that they cultivate their land by themselves. The table further reveals that relatively greater proportion (78%) of modern leaders engaged paid labourers than the traditional leaders (67%). The leaders who take the help of clan members constituted 12.5 per cent of the traditional leaders and 7 per cent of the modern leaders, and those who do it by themselves were 21 per cent and 27 per cent respectively. The analysis of the table reveals that though there is some variations in the responses of the leaders, it is too narrow to give a definite pattern in the mode of cultivation of the wet field land among the different types of leaders.

MODE OF ACQUISITION (WET FIELD LAND)

It is assumed that the study of mode of acquisition of the land would be helpful to understand the ascriptive aspect of the leadership, which hitherto, was an accepted proposition. The mode of acquisition was categorized as acquired, inherited and 'both' which means the land was inherited but it is developed and expanded by himself. The following table 3.13 shows the mode of acquisition of the land.

Table 3.13. Distribution of the Respondents According to the Mode of Acquisition of Their Land

Mode of acquisition	*Traditional leaders*				*Modern leaders*				
	GAM	*VE*	*PR*	*TL*	*PM*	*PL*	*CL*	*TL*	*G.TL*
Acquired	29 (50)	10 (40)	4 (67)	44 (49)	16 (40)	9 (36)	8 (38)	33 (38)	76 (43)
Inherited	6 (10)	4 (16)	1 (17)	12 (13)	5 (13)	8 (32)	4 (19)	17 (20)	28 (16)
Both	23 (40)	11 (44)	1 (17)	33 (37)	19 (48)	8 (32)	4 (43)	36 (42)	71 (41)
Total	58 (100)	25 (100)	6 (100)	89 (100)	40 (100)	25 (100)	21 (100)	86 (100)	175 (100)

Note : This table reflects the responses of 175 leaders who possess wet field land.

The table reveals that out of 175 leaders who have wet field land, 43 per cent were acquired, only 16 per cent were found to have inherited from their father. 41 per cent of them confessed that theirs were both acquired and inherited. This table reveals that in terms of land possession, the ascriptive aspect of the leadership is limited to some extent only. The table further shows that the greater proportion (49%) of the traditional leaders have acquired land when compared to the modern leaders (38%), but conversely, those who have inherited land constituted 13 per cent among the traditional leaders, whereas, it is 20 per cent among the modern leaders. But those who inherited the land but developed and expanded by themselves constituted 37 per cent among the traditional leaders and 42 per cent among the modern leaders. The further leader-wise break-up shows that the acquired land is 50 per cent among the *Gams*, 40 per cent among the village elders and 67 per cent among the priests. But in case of the modern leaders, it is 40 per cent among Panchayat member, 36 per cent among party leaders and 38 per cent among church leaders, which is comparatively lesser than that of the traditional leaders. This is basically due to the age factor because modern leaders are comparatively younger in age, so they had limited scope to acquire new land at present.

TYPE OF DWELLING HOUSE

The type of dwelling house of the leaders is considered as one of the reliable indicator of the leaders' socio-economic status because the author himself visited their house for interview. So, there was no scope for manipulation of facts by the respondents. During the course of interview, it was found that though the majority of the respondents lived in the traditional house, considerable number of leaders were living in the modern house like permanent (RCC) and semi-permanent type (SPT) house which clearly revealed their higher economic status in the village. The following table 3.14 shows the type of dwelling house of the leaders.

The tables reveals that 3 per cent of the leaders live in RCC houses, 10 per cent live in Semi-Permanent Type (SPT) house and 19 per cent in Ordinary Building Type (OBT) with

Table 3.14. Distribution of the Respondents Showing the Type of Their Dwelling House

	Traditional leaders				*Modern leaders*				
Type	*GAM*	*VE*	*PR*	*TL*	*PM*	*PL*	*CL*	*TL*	*G.TL*
RCC	N	1 (3)	N	1 (1)	3 (7)	2 (7)	N	5 (5)	6 (3)
SPT	9 (13)	2 (5)	N	11 (9)	3 (7)	5 (17)	2 (7)	10 (10)	21 (10)
OBT with tin	18 (26)	5 (13)	1 (11)	24 (21)	11 (24)	5 (17)	3 (11)	19 (18)	43 (19)
OBT without tin	43 (61)	30 (79)	8 (89)	81 (69)	29 (64)	18 (60)	23 (82)	70 (67)	151 (68)
Total	70 (100)	38 (100)	9 (100)	117 (100)	46 (100)	30 (100)	28 (100)	104 (100)	221 (100)

tin house which meant that total of 32 per cent of the leaders live in modern house. The leaders living in the traditional Galo house constitute 68 per cent only. The comparative study of the type of dwelling house of the leaders reveals that only 1 per cent of the traditional leaders and 5 per cent of the modern leaders lives in RCC house. Those who have SPT house are 9 per cent among the traditional leaders and 10 per cent among the modern leaders but slightly higher proportion of (21%) of traditional leaders lives in OBT with tin house when compared to the modern leaders (18%). Further, those who stay in the traditional Galo house were slightly higher among the traditional leaders (69%) when compared to the modern leaders (67%). Hence, the table does not reveal any significant trend, though it is evident that the proportion of the leaders who have modern house is slightly higher among the modern leaders when compared to the traditional leaders. But the analysis of the type of dwelling house reveals that most of the leaders are drawn from economically higher status group. Thus, this table reveals that there is positive co-relationship between economic status and leadership.

Besides socio-economic indices of the leaders discussed in this chapter, we have taken few other indicators of socio-economic status, which is traditionally relevant in Galo society. They are *Togu, Hurin-Namrin* and ready generosity on public occasions, which is explained below. They may be understood as traditional determinants of leadership.

TOGU

Togu is a grand marriage celebration of the Galos in which numbers of mithuns are sacrificed at a time. The number of mithun sacrificed ranges from two to twenty or thirty depending upon the ready availability of mithuns and consent of the brides' party. But, mere sacrifice of mithuns in the name of marriage party is not at all a *Togu. Togu,* in real sense, is accompanied by long process of rites and ritual which is an expensive and exhaustive affair. The initial decision to perform *Togu* is taken by the concern person, but his decision must be ratified by the priest through the divine examination of egg and chicken liver, otherwise, one

Table 3.15. Distribution of the Respondents Showing the *Togu* Performed by Them

Response	*Traditional leaders*				*Modern leaders*				
	GAM	*VE*	*PR*	*TL*	*PM*	*PL*	*CL*	*TL*	*G.TL*
Yes	43	18	5	66	20	13	13	46	112
	(61)	(47)	(56)	(56)	(43)	(43)	(46)	(44)	(51)
No	27	20	4	51	26	17	15	58	109
	(39)	(53)	(44)	(44)	(57)	(57)	(54)	(56)	(49)
Total	70	38	9	117	46	30	28	104	221
	(100)	(100)	(100)	(100;	(100)	(100)	(100)	(100)	(100)

cannot perform *Togu* even if he is capable to do so. The Galos who are converted to the Christianity also celebrate the *Togu* but theirs is not accompanied by requisite rites and rituals and hence, cannot be called *Togu* in real traditional perspective. Though *Togu* is a private affair, the entire village population is associated in the process. Without full cooperation from the village population, no one can perform *Togu* however rich he may be. So, performing a *Togu* is a cherished ambition of a traditional Galo man but everybody cannot perform it. Given the nature of celebration and expenditure involved in terms of cash and kind, a person who perform *Togu* earn name and fame in the eye of the village people.

During the course of interview, the leaders were asked, "Have you performed *Togu* in your lifetime?" and if yes, how many times?" Table 3.15 reveals the performances of *Togu* by the leaders.

The table reveals that 51 per cent of the leaders have performed *Togu* in their lifetime, which suggest that the majority of the leaders hailed from traditionally higher economic status. The traditional economic status is one of the important determinants of leadership in Galo society. Relatively greater proportion (56%) of the traditional leaders performed *Togu* when compared to the modern leaders (44%).

Further, leader-wise breakup of the response shows that the proportion of leaders who performed *Togu* was highest among the Gam (61%) followed by priest (56%) and village elders (47%), but it was 43 per cent each among the panchayat and party leaders, and 46 per cent among the church leader. Hence, we can assume that the traditional leaders are proportionately wealthier in term of indigenous items like cattle, *Adam-Tadok*, rice and millets that are indispensable items of the *Togu* celebration. Besides, the modern leaders are comparatively younger in age and many of them are yet to perform *Togu* in their name because their sons are yet to get married.

INTENSITY OF *TOGU* PERFORMED

The respondents were further asked about the number of

Table 3.16. Distribution of the Respondents Showing the Number of *Togu* Performed by Them

No. of *Togu(s)*	*Traditional leaders*				*Modern leaders*				
	GAM	*VE*	*PR*	*TL*	*PM*	*PL*	*CL*	*TL*	*G.TL*
Once	24 (56)	13 (72)	4 (80)	41 (62)	17 (85)	9 (69)	11 (85)	37 (80)	78 (70)
Twice	10 (23)	4 (22)	1 (20)	15 (23)	2 (10)	3 (23)	2 (15)	7 (15)	22 (20)
More	9 (21)	1 (6)	N	10 (15)	1 (5)	1 (18)	N	2 (4)	12 (11)
Total	43 (100)	18 (100)	5 (100)	66 (100)	20 (100)	13 (100)	13 (100)	46 (100)	112 (100)

Note : This table reveals the response of 112 leaders who performed *Togu*.

Togu(s) they have performed. *Togu*, being an expensive affair, is found to be difficult for an average individual to perform twice or thrice. The following table 3.16 shows the number of *Togu(s)* performed by the leaders.

As table 3.16 reveals, out of 112 leaders who have performed *Togu*, 70 per cent of them performed only once which suggest that performing a *Togu* is not an easy task. Even then, substantial number of leaders performed *Togu* for more than once. 20 per cent of them performed twice and 11 per cent of them performed more than twice. The leader-wise break-up reveals that greater proportion of the traditional leaders, in comparison to modern leaders, performed *Togu* more than once. The leaders who performed *Togu* twice is 23 per cent among the traditional leaders and 15 per cent among the modern leaders. The leaders who performed *Togu* more than twice is 15 per cent among the traditional leaders and 4 per cent among the modern leaders. The table further reveals that the proportion of leaders who performed *Togu* twice or more is highest among the *Gams* (23% and 21%) respectively, followed by the party leaders (23% and 18%) respectively. No priest or church leader performed *Togu* for more than two times. Thus, the overall analysis of the table reveals that the greater proportion of traditional leaders performed *Togu* with greater intensity, which suggests that the traditional leaders are proportionately wealthier in the traditional perspective than the modern leaders. It further reveals that *Togu* being a traditional ritual is gradually neglected, may be due to its expensive nature or due to the gradual decay in the traditional bondage. It also could be due to the influence of the agents of modernization, and/or due to the religious transition.

GENEROSITY

Generous people are always admired and appreciated in every society. They do come to the rescue of others at the time of need as well as whenever there is any social function or developmental activities are being organized. Such admiration and appreciation ultimately led to obedience. In Galo society, rich and generous people donate cash and kind

Table 3.17(a) : Distribution of Leaders as Per Their Generosity

Response	*Traditional leaders*				*Modern leaders*				*G.TL*
	GAM	*VE*	*PR*	*TL*	*PM*	*PL*	*CL*	*TL*	
Yes	53	23	5	81	34	22	22	78	159
	(76)	(61)	(56)	(69)	(74)	(73)	(79)	(75)	(72)
No	17	15	4	36	12	8	6	26	62
	(24)	(39)	(44)	(31)	(26)	(27)	(21)	(25)	(28)
Total	70	38	9	117	46	30	28	104	221
	(100)	(100)	(100)	(100)	(100)	(100)	(100)	(100)	(100)

on public occasions and such ready generosity makes them influential in the village and influence indeed is synonymous of leadership. In our interview, the respondents were asked, "Have you ever donated generously on public occasions? Their response is presented in the table 3.17*(a)* below and analyzed subsequently.

The table shows that 72 per cent of the leaders said 'yes', whereas only 28 per cent said that they did not donate anything worth mention. The comparative study of the table reveals that the 'yes' percentage is higher (75%) among the modern leaders than the traditional leaders (69%). Thus, it indicates that leaders should be generous to some extent otherwise he may invite public criticism. It is more so in the tribal communities, as there is a close relation among the members based on ethnic lines and community feelings. That is why; it was found that after panchayat election, each winner in the election organized the victory party. But, it is strange, nevertheless a fact that losers in the panchayat election too organized the so-called 'loser party' to keep his supporter in high spirit. Thus, ready generosity is an important aspect of leaders at the grassroots level. The leaders were further asked, "What did you usually donate?" The following table 3.17*(b)* displays the items donated by the leaders.

Mithun is the most valuable animal and the possession of mithun is a mark of wealth in Galo society. It is an indispensable item in marriage and festivals. It is also used as medium of exchange and mode of payment of fines and compensations. The price of a mithun, though not fixed, varies from Rs. 8000/- to Rs. 18,000/- depending upon the size and health. However, in the marriage process, it is usually priced at Rs. 10,000/-. The table reveals that 11 per cent of leaders donated mithuns on various occasions. The leaders who donated cow constitute 55 per cent and pig 44 per cent. 42 per cent of them donated 'others' which includes goat, fowl, local beer (*Poka*) and cash. Thus, the analysis reveals that generosity is an important aspect of leadership in the Galo society. The leader-wise break-up shows that percentage of mithun and cow donors are slightly higher

Table 3.17*(b)* : Distribution of the Respondents Showing the Items Donated by Them

	Traditional leaders				*Modern leaders*				
Items	*GAM*	*VE*	*PR*	*TL*	*PM*	*PL*	*CL*	*TL*	*G.TL*
Mithun	4 (8)	5 (22)	N	9 (11)	4 (12)	4 (18)	1 (5)	9 (12)	18 (11)
Cow	27 (51)	14 (61)	1 (20)	42 (52)	24 (71)	11 (50)	10 (45)	45 (58)	87 (55)
Pig	25 (47)	11 (48)	2 (40)	38 (47)	18 (53)	6 (20)	8 (36)	32 (41)	70 (44)
Other	22 (42)	8 (35)	2 (40)	32 (40)	15 (44)	7 (31)	13 (59)	35 (45)	67 (42)

Note : Total is not given as many respondents indicated to have donated more than one item.

(12% and 58%) respectively among the modern leaders when compared to the traditional leaders (11% and 52%) respectively. But the percentages of pig donors are greater among the traditional leaders (38%). Since modern leaders are comparatively younger in age, their career as leader is shorter than the career of the traditional leaders. Considering their length of career as leader, the modern leaders are more generous than the traditional leaders. We can also assume that emerging leadership is likely to donate more in days to come. It could be so, because, as party politics is entering more intensively into the rural arena, the leaders are supposed to maintain their support-base for future political benefit. Hence, the client-patronage relations are very systematically maintained. But, the present table does not reveal significant leader-wise shift in terms of their generosity.

POLITICAL SOCIALIZATION

Party Affiliation

The study of party affiliation of the leaders is important to understand the level of participation of leaders in the existing political process. It is also relevant from the socialization point of view. It is believed that political party is a significant agent of political socialization. It also increases the understanding, hold and linkage of the leaders with the other political leaders and functionaries. And politically conscious people are likely to be more capable to take leadership role in the present situation. This study will further reveal as to what extent the party politics has penetrated into the labyrinth of the traditional Galo society, which, until some years back, was not explored by any political party. The following table 3.18 shows the party affiliation of the leaders.

The table 3.18 shows that 74 per cent of the total respondents (leaders) were loyal to the Indian National Congress. It is also observed that usually the village level leaders have a tendency to remain with the party in power. So, party affiliation is not strong and static. There have been so many instances of opposition leaders joining the ruling party after assembly election. That is why; the Congress

Table 3.18. Distribution of the Respondents Showing their Party Affiliation

Name of the Party	*Traditional leaders*				*Modern leaders*				
	GAM	*VE*	*PR*	*TL*	*PM*	*PL*	*CL*	*TL*	*G.TL*
INC	57 (81)	22 (58)	9 (100)	88 (75)	33 (72)	20 (67)	22 (79)	75 (72)	163 (74)
BJP	1 (1)	2 (5)	N	3 (3)	2 (4)	1 (3)	N	3 (3)	6 (3)
AC	8 (11)	11 (29)	N	19 (16)	7 (15)	5 (17)	4 (14)	16 (15)	35 (16)
NCP	3 (4)	2 (5)	N	5 (4)	2 (4)	1 (3)	2 (7)	5 (5)	8 (4)
Other	1 (1)	1 (3)	N	2 (2)	2 (4)	3 (10)	N	5 (5)	7 (3)
Total	70 (100)	38 (100)	9 (100)	117 (100)	46 (100)	30 (100)	28 (100)	104 (100)	221 (100)

loyalist is exceptionally high because, the congress party remained in the power for quite some years. The principal opposition party in Arunachal politics *i.e.* the Arunachal Congress has only 16 per cent followed by NCP (4%) and BJP (3%). Thus, it is evident that all the leaders belong to one party or the other which suggest that leaders are politically active and conscious. The leader-wise break-up does not show any important shift in the party affiliation among the different types of leaders.

ELECTORAL CAMPAIGNING

It was assumed that the study of the role of the leaders in election campaign will further reveal the nature of their participation in the modern political system. It will also reveal leaders' adaptability and receptivity of the changes taking place in the ongoing political environment and their ability to swim with the present currents. The respondents were asked, "Did you campaign for any political party in the last Assembly election? Table 3.19 below shows their response in the form of 'Yes' or 'No'.

The table 3.19 reveals that 71 per cent of the leaders took part in electoral campaign in the last assembly election. 29 per cent conceded that they did not take part in the campaigning. It can be safely concluded that the leaders are politically active. The comparative analysis of the response reveals that the modern leaders are politically more active than the traditional leaders because the 'Yes' percentage is proportionately higher (76%) among the modern leader when compared to the traditional leaders (67%). The leader-wise break-up shows that the "Yes" percentage is 66 per cent among the Gam, 71 per cent among the village elders and 56 per cent among the priests, but, in case of the modern leaders, it is 85 per cent among the panchayat members, 80 per cent among the party leaders and 57% among the church leaders which is an exception. The 'No' percentage is highest among the priests (44%) and the church leaders (43%) but the least among the panchayat member (15%) and the party leaders (20%). The overall analysis of the table reveals that the modern leaders are emerging as more active participants in the present political

Table 3.19. Distribution of Respondents Showing Their Electoral Campaign

Response	*Traditional leaders*				*Modern leaders*				
	GAM	*VE*	*PR*	*TL*	*PM*	*PL*	*CL*	*TL*	*G.TL*
Yes	46	27	5	78	39	24	16	79	157
	(66)	(71)	(56)	(67)	(85)	(80)	(57)	(76)	(71)
No	24	11	4	39	7	6	12	25	64
	(34)	(29)	(44)	(33)	(15)	(20)	(43)	(24)	(29)
Total	70	38	9	117	46	30	28	104	221
	(100)	(100)	(100)	(100)	(100)	(100)	(100)	(100)	(100)

system. It also reveals that even the traditional leaders are attracted towards electoral campaign. It is so, as the *Gams* and priests are usually considered as influential people in the rural Arunachal and the people have reverence for their seniority and knowledge.

EXTENT OF CAMPAIGN AREA

The information regarding the extent of campaign area of the leader is important to know their level of influence and their capability to out-reach. Earlier, it was conceived that the influence of a leader, however effective he might be, confined to the village only because inter-village communication was very limited except on social occasions like marriage. The following table 3.20 highlights the extent of campaign area of leaders.

According to the table 3.20, 53 per cent of the leaders' campaigning area confined to village level only. 41 per cent campaigned up to block level and 6 per cent up to the district level. Thus, the table suggests that influence of the leaders is no more confined to the village only; their presence is felt across the villages too. The table further shows that greater proportion of the modern leaders campaign at the higher level. The proportion of leaders who campaigned up to block level is higher (48%) among the modern leaders when compared to the traditional leaders (33%). The traditional and modern leaders who campaign up to district level constituted 4 per cent and 9 per cent respectively. The proportion of the respondents who campaign up to block level was 51 per cent among the panchayat members, 58 per cent among the party leaders and 25 per cent among the church leaders. But, in case of the traditional leaders, it was 30 per cent among *Gams*, 41 per cent among the village elders and 20 per cent among the priests. The overall analysis of the above table shows that the modern leaders have wider area of influence in comparison to the traditional leaders. The influence of the modern leaders are no more confined to individual villages only, rather their presence is felt across the villages. The table 3.20 reveals that the modern leaders are extending their influence beyond the village, is in fact

Table 3.20. Distribution of the Respondents Showing the Extent of Electoral Campaign

Campaign area	*Traditional leaders*				*Modern leaders*				
	GAM	*VE*	*PR*	*TL*	*PM*	*PL*	*CL*	*TL*	*G.TL*
Village Level	30 (65)	15 (56)	4 (80)	49 (63)	15 (38)	8 (33)	11 (69)	34 (43)	83 (53)
Block Level	14 (30)	11 (41)	1 (20)	26 (23)	20 (51)	14 (58)	4 (25)	38 (48)	64 (41)
District Level	2 (4)	1 (3)	N	3 (4)	4 (10)	2 (8)	1 (6)	7 (9)	10 (6)
Total	46 (100)	27 (100)	5 (100)	78 (100)	39 (100)	24 (100)	16 (100)	79 (100)	157 (100)

Note : This table reflects the response of 157 leaders who took part in the election campaign.

conditioned by the increased facilities of the communication, higher level of education and more political stake.

FACTORS RESPONSIBLE FOR JOINING POLITICS

The respondents were asked, "What prompted you to join politics?" It was felt necessary to know their reasons for joining politics to further know the leader's commitment to public welfare and entry into the political arena. The following table (3.21) reveals the reasons for joining politics.

As the table 3.21 reveals, 75 per cent of the leaders joined politics to serve the society. However, during the course of interview, it was noticed that there was a tendency to conceal the actual reasons for joining politics by the leader, and hence substantial number of the respondents preferred social service as the reason. The leaders who joined politics for name and fame constituted only 2 per cent, whereas 8 per cent of leaders' involvements in the politics were encouraged by the family tradition. With certain degree of hesitation and confusion, 17 per cent of them conceded that they took active part in politics for personal gain in form of post in the panchayat bodies, benefit from government contract works, employment to the children and to get beneficiary of various rural development programmes. It further reveals that those who joined politics for social service were 71 per cent among the traditional leaders and 77 per cent among the modern leaders. Such difference may be attributed to relatively greater degree of honesty in response among the old leaders. Those who said 'name & fame' constituted 2 per cent each only and those with family tradition constituted 10 per cent and 6 per cent respectively. But the proportion of respondents who joined politics for personal gain constituted 17 per cent of the traditional leaders and 18 per cent of the modern leaders. The overall analysis of the table does not reveal significant difference in the response of the traditional and modern leaders.

MEMBERSHIP IN ORGANIZATION/ASSOCIATIONS

Of late, the Galo society is witnessing a proliferation of various organizations based on clan[13] solidarity. Since clan

13. See 'Introduction' for Clan.

Table 3.21. Distribution of the Respondents Showing the Reasons for Their Joining Politics

Reasons	*Traditional leaders*				*Modern leaders*				
	GAM	*VE*	*PR*	*TL*	*PM*	*PL*	*CL*	*TL*	*G.TL*
Social service	50 (74)	28 (74)	5 (56)	83 (71)	35 (76)	21 (70)	24 (86)	80 (77)	164 (75)
Name & fame	1 (1)	1 (3)	N	2 (2)	N	2 (7)	N	2 (2)	4 (2)
Family tradition	6 (9)	4 (11)	1 (11)	11 (10)	5 (11)	1 (3)	N	6 (6)	17 (18)
Personal gain	11 (16)	5 (13)	3 (33)	19 (17)	9 (20)	6 (20)	4 (14)	19 (18)	38 (17)

Note : Total is not given as some of them indicated more than one reasons.

members are spread over different villages, there is growing awareness among them to keep contact with one another. Another noticeable trend is the formation of increasing number of local welfare associations or unions whose jurisdiction usually confined to villages or the administrative circle. One can also witness a mushrooming of Christian churches in the villages and subsequent growth of association or union based on religion. The table 3.22 displays the membership of the leaders in various associations or unions.

The table 3.22 reveals that 82 per cent of the leaders have membership in various unions and associations, whereas 18 per cent do not have any such membership. 35 per cent of the leaders have membership in associations based on clan solidarity. The sense of clan solidarity is still held high among the leaders. 29 per cent of leaders were member of local organization or associations committed to strive for welfare of local area only. 19 per cent of leaders have membership in religious organization, which is basically the church organization, because 61 per cent of the Christian respondents had the membership in the religious organization. The leader-wise break-up of the table reveals that compared to modern leaders, larger proportion (38%) of traditional leaders have membership in clan association, it is 32 per cent among the *Gams*, 48 per cent among the village elders and 45 per cent among the priests whereas, it is 32 per cent among the modern leaders *i.e.* 33 per cent among the panchayat member, 30% among the party leaders and 32 per cent among the church leaders. But, in local welfare associations, the modern leaders have larger proportion (32%) of membership—it is 41 per cent among panchayat members, 40 per cent among party leaders and 7 per cent among the church leaders, but it is 27 per cent among the traditional leaders *i.e.* 27 per cent among *Gam*, 29 per cent among the village elder and 22 per cent among the priests. Thus, it is revealed that in comparison to the traditional leaders, greater percentages of the emerging leadership are members of the secular organization. On the other hand, the traditional leaders have greater percentage of membership in clan-based

Table 3.22. Distribution of the Respondents Showing Their Membership in Associations or Unions

Unions/Assn.	Traditional leaders				Modern leaders				
	GAM	*VE*	*PR*	*TL*	*PM*	*PL*	*CL*	*TL*	*G.TL*
Clan Assn.	22 (31)	18 (47)	4 (44)	44 (37)	15 (32)	9 (30)	9 (32)	33 (32)	77 (35)
Local Welfare Assn.	18 (27)	11 (29)	2 (22)	31 (26)	19 (41)	12 (40)	2 (7)	33 (32)	64 (29)
Religious Orgn.	9 (14)	6 (16)	N	15 (13)	5 (11)	4 (13)	17 (61)	26 (25)	41 (19)
Nil	21 (30)	3 (8)	3 (33)	27 (23)	7 (15)	5 (17)	N	12 (11)	39 (18)
Total	70 (100)	38 (100)	9 (100)	117 (100)	46 (100)	30 (100)	28 (100)	104 (100)	221 (100)

organization. So, the analysis shows that the emerging leaders are more secular and modern in their institutional affiliation. It also points to the fact that the emerging leaders are preferably consulted on the contemporary issues of general interest.

EXPOSURE TO MASS MEDIA

Many studies have proved that exposure to the mass media such as radio, newspapers and contact with the agents of change is also an indication of linkage with the external system. Exposure to these sources of information facilitates progressive orientation and brings about a change in social outlook. The people who regularly read newspaper and listen to the radio are likely to possess better knowledge of the current affairs relating to various problems and issues. The exposures to the means of mass communication like radio and newspapers have definite impact on the value perception and orientation of the leaders. Hence, to analyze the leaders' exposure to mass media, they were asked, "Do you listen to radio?" Their response is presented in table 3.23.

Due to the lack of transport facilities, the print media is yet to be commonly available in the rural villages. Thus, the radio was found to be the most popular and accessible mass media for the rural population. The table 3.23 reveals that with an exception of 12 per cent who do not listen to the radio, the rest listens to the radio regularly or occasionally. The table reveals that 50 per cent of the leaders listen to radio occasionally and 38 per cent listen regularly which means that 88 per cent of the total respondents have access to the radio. The comparative analysis of the table reveals that the percentage of leaders who listen to the radio regularly was proportionately higher among the modern leaders (44%) than the traditional leaders (33%). The leader-wise regular listener among the modern leaders was 43 per cent among the Panchayat members, 47 per cent among the party leaders and 43 per cent among the Church leaders whereas, in case of the traditional leaders, the regular listener constitute 31 per cent among the *Gams*, 43 per cent among the village elders and 11 per cent among the priests. But those who never listen to radio were proportionately

Table 3.23. Distribution of the Respondents Showing their Access to Radio

Response	*Traditional leaders*				*Modern leaders*				
	GAM	*VE*	*PR*	*TL*	*PM*	*PL*	*CL*	*TL*	*G.TL*
Never listen	9	7	4	20	1	3	2	6	26
	(13)	(18)	(44)	(17)	(2)	(10)	(7)	(6)	(12)
Listen occasionally	39	15	4	58	13	13	14	52	110
	(56)	(39)	(44)	(50)	(43)	(43)	(50)	(50)	(50)
Listen regularly	22	16	1	39	14	14	12	46	85
	(31)	(43)	(11)	(33)	(47)	(43)	(43)	(44)	(38)
Total	70	38	9	117	30	30	28	104	221
	(100)	(100)	(100)	(100)	(100)	(100)	(100)	(100)	(100)

Table 3.24. Distribution of the Respondents Showing Their Preference of Programmes

Response	*Traditional leaders*				*Modern leaders*				
	GAM	*VE*	*PR*	*TL*	*PM*	*PL*	*CL*	*TL*	*G.TL*
News	27	21	2	50	39	19	15	73	123
	(44)	(68)	(40)	(52)	(86)	(70)	(58)	(75)	(63)
Entertainment	1	1	N	2	1	1	5	7	9
	(2)	(3)		(2)	(2)	(4)	(19)	(7)	(5)
Cultural	33	9	3	45	5	7	6	18	63
(*Nyitom Ponu*)	(54)	(29)		(46)	(11)	(26)	(23)	(18)	(32)
Total	61	31	5	97	45	27	26	98	195
	(100)	(100)	(100)	(100)	(100)	(100)	(100)	(100)	(100)

Note : This table reflects the opinion of 195 leaders who listen to radio.

higher among the traditional leaders (17%) when compared to the modern leaders (6%). The leader-wise percentage who never listen to radio constitute 9 per cent of *Gam*, 7 per cent of village elders and 44 per cent of the priests but, in case of modern leaders, it is 2 per cent of Panchayat member, 10 per cent of party leaders and 7 per cent of the Church leaders. Hence, the emerging leaders are likely to be more conscious and aware of the new developments taking place in the society because they have, as table reveals, better access to the radio more frequently.

PREFERENCE OF RADIO PROGRAMMES

To know the leaders' preference of radio programme, they were asked, "Which programme do you like most?" Their response is presented in 3.24.

The table reveals that majority (63%) of the leaders preferred to listen news. This suggests that the leaders are keen to learn about what is happening in the present day world. They are likely to be aware of the developments taking place in the society. Only 5 per cent of the respondents preferred to listen to entertainment programmes like songs and dramas. The considerable percentage (32%) of the leaders listen to cultural programmes or *Nyitom Ponu i.e.* hymns, narration and rhapsodies of the stories and legends broadcasted in local dialect. The leader-wise break-up of the programme preference reveals that the modern leaders are more interested in listening to news but on the other hand, the traditional leaders are more interested in listening to the cultural programmes. The proportion of leaders who prefers to listen to news constituted 74.50 per cent among the modern leaders but 52 per cent among the traditional leaders. The leader-wise percentage of news listener among the modern leaders are 86 per cent among the Panchayat members, 70 per cent among the party leaders and 58 per cent among the Church leader, but in case of traditional leader, the news listener is 44 per cent among the *Gams*, 68 per cent among the village elders and 40 per cent among the priests. On the other hand, the leaders who preferred cultural programmes were 46 per cent among the traditional leaders but 18 per cent among the modern leaders. The

Table 3.25. Distribution of the Respondents Showing Their Access to Newspaper

Response	*Traditional leaders*				*Modern leaders*				*G.TL*
	GAM	*VE*	*PR*	*TL*	*PM*	*PL*	*CL*	*TL*	
Don't read	20 (83)	11 (46)	N	31 (65)	17 (50)	11 (44)	16 (67)	44 (53)	75 (57)
Occasionally	4 (17)	13 (54)	N	17 (35)	17 (50)	14 (56)	8 (33)	39 (47)	56 (43)
Regularly	N	N	N	N	N	N	N	N	N
Total	24 (100)	24 (100)	N	48 (100)	34 (100)	25 (100)	24 (100)	83 (100)	131 (100)

Note : This table reflects the response of 131 literate leaders.

leader-wise proportion of respondents who preferred cultural programme are 54 per cent, 29 per cent and 60 per cent respectively among *Gams*, village elders and the priest but in case modern leaders, it is 11 per cent, 26 per cent and 23 per cent respectively among the Panchayat members, party leader and the Church leaders. The proportion of respondents who preferred entertainment programme is also higher (7%) among the modern leaders when compared to the 2 per cent of the traditional leaders. By considering the leader-wise proportion of news listener, we can safely derive that the emerging leaders are likely to have better awareness and knowledge of the contemporary situation when compared to the traditional leaders.

ACCESS TO NEWSPAPER

To know more about the leaders' exposure to mass media, we asked them a question regarding their access to newspapers, "Do you read newspapers?" Their response is presented in table 3.25 below :

The table reveals that the majority (57%) of the leaders do not read newspaper. This is mainly because of two important reasons. Firstly, there is rare circulation of newspapers in the villages due to communication bottlenecks. Secondly, in our study, the literate leaders include those who can simply write and sign his name. Many of them do not properly understand the contents of the newspaper because almost half (43%) of the literate leaders studied up to primary level only. The table further shows that 43 per cent of the leaders read newspaper occasionally. These leaders belong to the village, which fall in the foothill area bordering Assam or nearby administrative centre or sub-centre or those who, very often, visit the towns for various purposes. The comparative study of the responses in the table reveals that the proportion of newspaper reader is higher among the modern leaders (47%) in comparison to the traditional leaders (35%). The leader-wise newspaper reader, though occasional, among the modern leaders is 50 per cent among Panchayat member, 56 per cent among the party leader and 33 per cent among the Church leaders but in case of traditional leaders, it is 17 per cent among *Gams*,

54 per cent among the village elder and no priest reads newspaper because all were illiterate. None of the respondents read newspaper regularly. Thus, we can assume that the modern leaders are likely to be more aware and better exposed to the outside world because they are relatively better exposed to newspapers.

SUMMARY

The analysis of the responses of the respondents to the questionnaire reveals that the socio-economic background of an individual has important bearing on the emergence of leadership. It also reveals that perceptible change has taken place in the leadership phenomenon because; many of the traditionally important determinants of leadership are proved to have outlived its utility. The variables like age, occupation, income and the large family size are no more the important ingredients of leadership. The substantial proportions of the leaders were drawn from the younger generation and small family size. The income of the leaders in terms of rupees was negligible. Sex and educational background was found to be important determinants of leadership. The emerging leadership was found to have relatively greater proportion of female and literate leaders among them when compared to the traditional leaders. The economic status as indicated by property, land, type of dwelling house, generosity on public occasions and *Togu* celebration was found to be the important determining factors of leadership, but the leader-wise variation was evident in these variables. The trends of changes in the leadership were also found in the variables like income source, mode of land holding, type of dwelling house, *Togu* celebration, electoral campaigning and the membership in the unions and associations etc. The emerging leadership was found to be more literate, secular, generous and active participants in the modern political system when compared to the traditional leaders. The study further shows that though not regularly, the leaders had satisfactory exposure to the mass media like radio and newspaper. The modern leaders are better exposed to the mass media in comparison to the traditional leaders. Hence, it could be drawn that the modern leaders are having better political socialization, and are drawn from better socio-economic back-ground in comparison to the traditional leaders.

4

Attitudes, Perceptions and Awareness of the Leaders

The attitudes, perceptions and the level of awareness of the leaders are reflective of the changes taking place in the society. The attitude and subsequent thinking process of leaders about the issues of socio-cultural importance have special significance due to the fact that the leaders in any society are the precursors to change and hence, leaders' perception become the perception of the masses in course of time. "The change in the value-orientation of the leadership, therefore, might throw some light on the essential nature of changes taking place in that society"[1]. The perception of the leaders may create obstacles in the path of desired changes or may facilitate such changes. It is assumed that under the humanizing impact of state-sponsored programmes and general modernizing factors, there has been considerable changes in leader's attitude and perception on some important socio-cultural issues like child-marriage, women's status, existing taboos, etc. At the same time, it is also assumed that there has been significant change in the status of the traditional authority and their hold over the common people in the village.

To assess the attitudes and perceptions of the leaders, some specific questions regarding the issues of socio-cultural importance concerning the Galo society were forwarded to the respondents. Further, their opinion on

1. Choudhary, D.S., *Emerging Rural Leadership in an Indian State*, Manthan Publication, Delhi, 1981, p. 90.

contemporary state of the *Keba* and its leadership were sought. The present chapter is an attempt to comprehend the attitude of the leaders pertaining to certain vital issues therein and their understanding about the possible solutions to those issues.

INTER-TRIBAL MARRIAGE

In earlier days, the activities of the Galos were confined mostly to village only. The village was an independent unit itself. There was hardly any contact with other villages except for occasions like marriage. The other reason for such secluded life was the lack of transport facilities and general outlook of the people. Hence, chances of inter-tribal marriage did not arise then, even though the society did not disapprove of such marriage. The marriage area usually confined to nearby villages of other clans or within a village if people of different clans live together. The marriage within the clan members[2] is considered incestuous and hence, strictly prohibited. But the increasing network of transport facilities and growing awareness of the people has facilitates regular contact with one another. Now, not only inter-tribal marriage but also marriages with non-tribals are not looked at as an aberration, especially among the educated and urbanized section of the Galo society, but it is still a rare phenomenon in the rural areas. Hence, to know the leaders' opinion on inter-tribal marriage, they were asked, "Do you like inter-tribe marriage?" Their response is presented in table 4.1.

The table shows that majority (66%) of the leaders like inter-tribe marriage. They expressed that as the society is becoming more progressive; where the children are exposed to modern way of life, intend to have their liberty to choose their partners. Further, during the course of interview, many respondents confessed that they do not have sufficient control over their school and college going children about their marriage. But 34 per cent of the leaders said that they do not like the inter-tribe marriage. Even then, it is noticeable that leaders' opinions on this particular question

2. See 'Profile of the Galos' for Clans.

Table 4.1. Distribution of Respondents Showing Their Opinion on Inter-Tribal Marriage

Response	*Traditional leaders*				*Modern leaders*				
	GAM	*VE*	*PR*	*TL*	*PM*	*PL*	*CL*	*TL*	*G.TL*
Yes	43	28	5	76	32	20	18	70	146
	(61)	(74)	(56)	(65)	(70)	(67)	(64)	(67)	(66)
No	27	10	4	41	14	10	10	34	75
	(39)	(26)	(44)	(35)	(30)	(33)	(36)	(33)	(34)
Total	70	38	9	117	46	30	28	104	221
	(100)	(100)	(100)	(100)	(100)	(100)	(100)	(100)	(100)

are in conformity with the changing trends. The leader-wise break-up of the response shows that though not very significant, the emerging leaders are more broad-minded and secular in their outlook because 'no' percentage is slightly higher (35%) among the traditional leaders, it is 39 per cent among *Gams*, 26 per cent among the village elders and 44% among the priests. But in case of modern leaders, the 'no' percentage is 32 per cent constituting 30 per cent among the Panchayat member, 33 per cent among the party leaders and 36 per cent among the Church leaders.

TYPES OF MARRIAGE

The marriage systems of the Galos are sometimes simple but at some other times complex too. Practically, there are four types of marriage systems, some of which are now discarded. The first is the *'Neppe Nyida'*[3] *i.e.* a system of marriage in advance when the child is still in mother's womb. This system of marriage has died a natural death. The second type is the 'child marriage'. The marriage is solemnized during the childhood of the prospective couples. The third is the 'negotiated marriage'. In case of negotiated marriage, the elders or parents of the potential groom look for a bride and the marriage is negotiated accordingly. This is still a popular practice. The fourth type is the 'marriage by choice' or popularly known as 'love-marriage' where the elders and parents do not play a role in selecting a bride or a groom. This is the present trend, which is very popular in the Galo society. Thus, the leaders were asked, "What type of marriage do you prefer for your son and daughter?" Their response is presented in table 4.2 below.

The table reveals that no leader, except one *Gam*, prefers child marriage because leaders were aware of the problems arising out of child marriage. There have been many instances of breaking down of child-married couples and dispute ensued over the settlement of 'give and take' that accompanied the process of marriage. The most preferred marriage system is the 'marriage by choice' (74%) but considerable proportion (26%) of leaders still preferred

3. See 'Profile of the Galos' for Marriage.

Table 4.2. Distribution of the Respondents Showing Their Preference of Types of Marriage

Response	*Traditional leaders*				*Modern leaders*				
	GAM	*VE*	*PR*	*TL*	*PM*	*PL*	*CL*	*TL*	*G.TL*
Child Marriage	1 (1)	N	N	1 (0)	N	N	N	N	1 (0)
Arranged Marriage	18 (26)	9 (24)	3 (33)	30 (26)	12 (26)	8 (27)	7 (25)	27 (26)	57 (26)
Marriage by choice	51 (73)	29 (76)	6 (67)	86 (74)	34 (74)	22 (73)	21 (75)	77 (74)	163 (74)
Total	70 (100)	38 (100)	9 (100)	117 (100)	46 (100)	30 (100)	28 (100)	104 (100)	221 (100)

Note : Percentages are given in the brackets.

'arranged marriage' for their sons and daughters. The leader-wise break-up does not reveal any significant variation in the responses of the different types of leaders because those who preferred 'arranged marriage' were 26 per cent each among the traditional and the modern leaders, and those who preferred 'marriage by choice' were also 74 per cent each. But, the overall picture of the table reveals that the leaders opinion on types of marriage is in tune with the present popular trend.

NYAME GINAM OR *NYAME RENAM*

Nyame Ginam[4] *i.e.* 'sexual relationship with the brothers' wife' is a strange traditional practice among the Galos. Such relationship extends to the clan brothers (*Sitem*) also. This system is being increasingly denounced by the progressive Galos themselves but society as a whole do not consider such relationship as incestuous or a taboo. But, it is wrong to believe that all the brothers or the clan brothers have sexual right over brother's wife. It is neither a right nor obligatory on the part of the wife to entertain them. Such relationship depends on their mutual understanding, personal intimacy and the tacit consent of the actual husband. "Whatever might be the draw-back of this custom, its merits are greater than demerits"[5]. In our interview schedule, the respondents (leaders) were asked, " Do you like the practice of '*Nyame Ginam*' in your society?" Their opinion is presented in table 4.3.

The tables reveal that 30 per cent of the grassroots leaders favoured the retention of the system but 49 per cent considered it as derogatory and hence, do not like the practice of *Nyame Ginam*. The leaders who favoured the system had their own version of justification of the practice. The system had number of merits in the traditional hunting and agricultural practices. It is also an expression of solidarity, love and affection amongst the brother in-laws and sister in-laws in the Galo joint family. The distribution of her favours among all brothers without discrimination

4. See 'Profile of Galos' for details.
5. Nyori, Tai, *History and Culture of the Adis*, Omsons Publications, New Delhi, 1993, p. 246.

Table 4.3. Distribution of the Respondents Showing Their Opinion on *Nyame Ginam*

	Traditional leaders				*Modern leaders*				
Responses	*GAM*	*VE*	*PR*	*TL*	*PM*	*PL*	*CL*	*TL*	*G.TL*
Yes	22 (31)	16 (42)	3 (33)	41 (35)	14 (30)	6 (20)	5 (18)	25 (24)	66 (30)
No	32 (46)	16 (42)	3 (33)	51 (44)	20 (43)	19 (63)	19 (68)	58 (56)	109 (49)
To some extent	16 (23)	6 (16)	3 (33)	25 (21)	12 (26)	5 (17)	4 (14)	21 (20)	46 (21)
Total	70 (100)	38 (100)	9 (99)	117 (100)	46 (100)	30 (100)	28 (100)	104 (100)	221 (100)

was once considered as highly commendable feminine virtue. But as the table reveals, 49 per cent of the respondents said that they don't like the system, 21 per cent of them expressed solidarity with the system but with strong reservations. Thus, it is revealed that the majority of the leaders do not like the system but it is not easy to completely wipe out the custom, which is practiced since times immemorial. The leader-wise break-up of the response reveals that the 'Yes' percentage is higher among the traditional leaders (35%) than the modern leaders (24%) but, it is reverse in the case of who said 'No'. The 'Yes' percentage among the traditional leaders are 31 per cent among the *Gams*, 42 per cent among the village elders and 33 per cent among the priests, whereas, in case of the modern leaders, it is 30.43 per cent among the panchayat members, 20 per cent among party leaders and 17.85 per cent among the church leaders. It shows that the traditional leaders are comparatively more conservative and tradition bound in their outlook and opinion than the modern leaders. However, the shift in leaders outlook is clearly evident. There is general tendency to give up the derogatory social practice like *Nyame Ginam* and the emerging leaders are more progressive in their outlook in this connection.

BRIDE-PRICE *(OMEH AREH)*

In contrast to the dowry practice prevalent in other societies in India, the system of 'bride price' is unique by itself in case of the Galo society. Unlike the other societies, in Galo society, the parents of the bridegroom pay to the bride's parent, which is called *'Omeh Areh'*. Traditional rate of *'Omeh Areh'*, *i.e.* 'bride price' in Galo society is usually two mithuns and excess, if any, is to be paid back by the bride's family in the form of beads and bowls *(Adam Tadok)* in rough proportion. The description like bride price may convince the distant observer to think that women are sold and bought like a property in the Galo society. But that is not exactly the case. It is usually noticed that the groom's party is always interested to give but the brides' party refuse or reluctantly accept the offer because the later has to pay back in form of *Adam Tadok*. Thus, if we analyze this long process of 'give

Table 4.4. Distribution of the Respondents Showing Their Opinion on Bride-Price

	Traditional leaders				Modern leaders				
Response	*GAM*	*VE*	*PR*	*TL*	*PM*	*PL*	*CL*	*TL*	*G.TL*
Yes	30 (43)	15 (39)	4 (44)	49 (42)	12 (26)	6 (20)	8 (20)	26 (25)	75 (34)
No	19 (27)	11 (29)	2 (22)	32 (27)	20 (43)	9 (30)	11 (39)	40 (38)	72 (33)
To some extent	21 (30)	12 (32)	3 (33)	36 (31)	14 (31)	15 (30)	9 (32)	38 (37)	74 (33)
Total	70 (100)	38 (100)	9 (100)	117 (100)	46 (100)	30 (100)	28 (100)	104 (100)	221 (100)

and take' between two families from the 'profit-loss' point of view, the groom's party is a gainer and the brides' party, a loser. There are relative merits and demerits of the practice. For the purpose of our study, the respondents were asked, "Do you like the system of bride-price *(Omeh Areh)*?" Their response is presented in table 4.4 below :

The table reveals a clearly divided opinion among the leaders. The 34 per cent of the leaders like the system of bride price whereas 33 per cent do not like the same. Another 33 per cent have reservation either to retain it or reject it. They like the system of bride price to some extent only. But, if we add the 'yes' percentage and the percentage of leaders who like it with some reservation, the implicit or explicit supporter outnumber the leaders who dislike the system. Hence, analysis of the overall response reveals that it is not easy to do away with the customary practices, but attitudinal changes among the leaders is clearly reflected. The leader-wise break-up of the response reveals that the 'no' percentage is higher among the modern leaders (38%) when compared to the traditional leaders (27%). The leaders who do not like the system of bride price is 43 per cent among the Panchayat members, 30 per cent among the party leaders and 39 per cent among the Church leaders, but in case of traditional leaders, it is 27 per cent among the *Gam*, 29 per cent among the village elders and 22 per cent among the priests. So, there is difference in value perception between the traditional and modern leaders. The later is more progressive and rational in their outwork.

TOGU

Togu[6], a grand marriage celebration among the Galos is an auspicious occasion. The number of mithuns sacrificed in a *Togu* varies from two to twenty and at times thirty. But actual customary rules prescribe ten mithuns is sufficient to propitiate the concern deities. Thus, sacrificing of more than ten mithuns in a *Togu* may be considered as mere display of economic might. Of late, there is a tendency among the rich people to sacrifice 25 to 30 mithuns in a *Togu*, which has endangered its existence in the Galo area. The largest

6. See 'Chapter-III' for *Togu*.

Table 4.5. Distribution of the Respondents Showing Their Opinion on Slaughtering of Mithuns in a *Togu*

Response	*Traditional leaders*				*Modern leaders*				
	GAM	*VE*	*PR*	*TL*	*PM*	*PL*	*CL*	*TL*	*G.TL*
Yes	18 (26)	6 (16)	2 (22)	26 (22)	4 (9)	6 (20)	1 (4)	11 (11)	37 (17)
No	32 (46)	19 (50)	3 (33)	54 (46)	28 (61)	21 (70)	14 (50)	63 (61)	117 (53)
To some extent	20 (29)	13 (34)	4 (44)	37 (32)	14 (30)	3 (10)	13 (46)	30 (29)	67 (30)
Total	70 (100)	38 (100)	9 (100)	117 (100)	46 (100)	30 (100)	28 (100)	104 (100)	221 (100)

number of mithuns sacrificed in a single *Togu* recorded by the author was 40 mithuns. So, slaughtering of mithuns in marriage ceremony has become an issue in the Galo society, especially among the educated and enlightened groups. Thus, the leaders were asked, "Do you like the slaughtering of large numbers of mithuns in a marriage ceremony *(Togu)*?" Their response is presented in table 4.5.

The table reveals that only 17 per cent of the leaders favour the system of sacrificing large number of mithuns in a *Togu* but majority (53%) of the leaders oppose the slaughtering. They were conscious of the fact that if the present trend of slaughtering of mithuns continue, it will become an endangered spices and cost of the mithuns will increase automatically, in which case, an average person will be in difficulty, as mithuns are being used for many purposes as medium of exchange, source of income, mode of payment of compensation and fines etc. Further, 30 per cent of the respondents favour the system to some extent only. Most of them conceded that number of mithuns sacrificed in a *Togu* should not exceed ten. Many of them favoured the fixation of upper limit for numbers of mithuns to be sacrificed in a marriage ceremony. Thus, it is evident that the leaders are conscious of the disadvantage of the slaughtering of mithuns in a marriage ceremony, which indicates a progressive orientation on the part of the leaders. The leader-wise break-up shows that the proportion of 'no' percentage is higher among the modern leaders (61%) in comparison to the traditional leaders (46%). The leader-wise break-up was 61 per cent among Panchayat members, 70 per cent among the party leaders and 50 per cent among the Church leaders. But in case of traditional leaders, the 'no' percentage was 46 per cent among the *Gams*, 50 per cent among village elders and 33 per cent among the priest. Those who favoured the system constituted 22 per cent among the traditional leaders but 11 per cent among the modern leaders. The 'yes' percentage was the highest among the *Gams* (26%) and the lowest among the Church leaders (4%). Thus, the emerging leaders are more progressive and rational in their outlook than the traditional leaders in this question.

SOCIAL TABOOS OR RESTRICTIONS

The Galos observe innumerable types of taboos or restrictions from childhood to death. Some of these taboos are general and some are contextual and specific. There are so many do's and don'ts' to be separately observed by young people, expected mother and her husband, patients after rituals, those who killed a tiger, one bitten by snake, one who carried dead body, nephew, new brides, hunters, priest and so on. The taboos are so complex and diverse that it is almost impossible to give a vivid picture of different types of taboos, mode of following them and who are to observe what kind of taboos. All the taboos are not necessarily observed now but, everyone, even the young people are aware of these taboos because they have learnt it from their elders and parents since childhood. To give some example of the taboos—*(i)* a female member cannot enter the house through front during the menstrual period. The prominent reason for such restriction is that martial spirit of the male members in hunting and fishing may get diminished, *(ii)* the husband of pregnant woman should not tie a knot or fix a permanent post otherwise she will get problem in delivery, *(iii)* the children should not eat brain, tongue, and heart of the animals otherwise his future potentiality of being a leader *(Nyijik Nyikok)* will be diminished, *(iv)* a person bitten by snake should stay in nearby jungle for at least two to three nights, and no one should take anything from the victim's house for certain period of time otherwise, similar snake biting case may occur to those who do not observe the restrictions and so on. It is observed that some of the taboos are no more followed but some are still retained. The severity of the taboos also differs in different cases and areas. In our interview schedule, the leaders were asked, "Do you think that existing social taboos or restrictions are relevant in the modern context"? Their response is presented in table 4.6 below :

The table reveals that only 15 per cent of the leaders considered the existing taboos as relevant but majority (53%) of the respondents said that the existing taboos are not relevant in the present context. They do not find any logic

Table 4.6. Distribution of the Respondents Showing Their Opinion on Existing Social Taboos

Response	*Traditional leaders*				*Modern leaders*				
	GAM	*VE*	*PR*	*TL*	*PM*	*PL*	*CL*	*TL*	*G.TL*
Relevant	16 (23)	6 (16)	5 (56)	27 (23)	4 (9)	2 (7)	N	6 (6)	33 (15)
Not relevant	40 (57)	15 (39)	1 (11)	56 (48)	23 (50)	17 (57)	21 (75)	61 (59)	117 (53)
Relevant to some extent	14 (20)	17 (45)	3 (33)	34 (29)	19 (41)	11 (37)	7 (25)	37 (36)	71 (32)
Total	70 (100)	38 (100)	9 (100)	117 (100)	46 (100)	30 (100)	28 (100)	104 (100)	221 (100)

or justification behind these taboos. But certain proportion (32 per cent) of the leaders said that some of the social taboos are relevant and some are irrelevant. They said that some does and don'ts in the society must be retained as a part of our traditional practices. The overall picture reveals that the progressives ones outnumbered the conservatives and neutrals, and hence significant proportion of leaders have abandoned their traditional values and moores due to their exposure to outside world. But some of them still hover around the traditionalism, which is a significant feature of the transitional societies. The comparative analysis of the response shows that the new leaders are comparatively more rational and scientific in their outlook than the traditional leaders. The proportion of the leaders, who considered the existing taboos as relevant are higher among the traditional leaders (23%), when compared to the modern leaders (6%). The leader-wise break-up of the respondents who considered the existing taboos as relevant was 23 per cent among the *Gam*, 16 per cent among the village elders and 56 per cent among the priests, but in case of modern leaders, it is 9 per cent among the Panchayat members, 7 per cent among the party leaders and no Church leader considered the social taboos as relevant due to their separate belief system. But in case of the leaders who said that the taboos are irrelevant, it is just the reverse. The leaders who considered irrelevant is proportionately higher among the modern leaders (59%) when compared to the traditional leaders (48%). The respondent who said 'relevant' was highest among the priests (56%) followed by the *Gam* (23%). One significant aspect of the analysis is that 25 per cent of the Church leader still considers that some taboos are relevant which shows that the traditional belief system still holds importance inspite of the changing environment. But, the overall picture of the above table reveals a definite shift in value-orientation and perceptions of the leaders in Galo society.

PREFERENCE OF CHILD

Usually, a Galo man prefers male child because his genealogical chain is continued through the male only. The

Galos strongly believe in the sanctity of genealogy and every Galo individual is suppose to know the genealogical route of origin right from *Abotani*[7] down to himself and any deletion in the chain is considered inauspicious and may be looked down in the society. Such genealogical continuity could be maintained due to the peculiar system of naming a person. Galo men always prefix the second syllable of his father's name in his own name and system continues down the generation. This is one of the main reasons why a Galo usually prefer a male child. It was assumed that leader's preference of male or female child would throw a light on gender sensitization in the Galo society and relative rigidity and flexibility in their traditional outlook. Hence, the leaders were asked, "What child do you prefer first?" Their response is presented in table 4.7 :

As the table reveals, the majority (56%) of the leaders preferred male child, which is a clear reflection of traditional patriarchal society. However, significant numbers (15%) of leaders were progressive enough to prefer girl child, but 29 per cent of them did not take rigid stand on the issue. They had no specific preference over the sex of child. The leaders who preferred female child and who do not have specific preference constituted 44 per cent and it is very significant considering the sanctity attached to genealogical continuity and the nature of patriarchal society. The leader-wise break-up of the table reveals that the percentage of leaders who preferred female child is slightly larger among the modern leader (18%) when compared to the traditional leaders (12%). 53 per cent and 58 per cent respectively preferred male child. Hence, the proportionate difference in the pattern of response between the modern and traditional leaders is not wide enough for meaningful generalization but, as the table reveals, the modern leaders were relatively more liberal than the traditional leaders. The overall picture of the leaders' preferences of child reveals a change in the leaders' outlook though not very significant in this particular question. Many traditional moorings attached to the status of women are sinking in the waves of present environment. Many leaders confessed that usually daughters are better

7. See 'Introduction' for details.

Table 4.7. Distribution of the Respondents Showing Their Preference of Child

Response	*Traditional leaders*				*Modern leaders*				
	GAM	*VE*	*PR*	*TL*	*PM*	*PL*	*CL*	*TL*	*G.TL*
Son	42	22	4	68	26	17	12	55	123
	(60)	(58)	(44)	(58)	(57)	(57)	(43)	(53)	(56)
Daughter	9	4	1	14	6	6	7	19	33
	(13)	(11)	(11)	(12)	(13)	(20)	(25)	(18)	(15)
No specific	19	12	4	35	14	7	9	30	65
	(27)	(32)	(44)	(40)	(30)	(23)	(32)	(29)	(29)
Total	70	38	9	117	46	30	28	104	221
	(100)	(100)	(100)	(100)	(100)	(100)	(100)	(100)	(100)

because daughters have longer emotional attachment with the parents and help the parents with cash or kind at regular intervals even after the marriage. Before marriage also, girl child gives regular assistance to the parents in domestic household activities. So, many leaders confessed that they prefer son only to maintain the genealogical chain of origin.

PREFERENCE OF EDUCATION TO CHILDREN

As stated earlier, the Galo society is truly a patriarchal society and it will not be surprising if there is any biasness against the female child in the matter of giving formal education. Since women reservation in the Panchayat bodies were implemented in the Panchayat election of April 2003 throughout Arunachal Pradesh, the message of women empowerment has reached the villages also. It was assumed that the leader's preference of giving education to male or female child would throw light on their perception about the status of women in the socio-political system. Hence, the leaders were asked, "Whose education, do you consider, is more important?" Their response is presented in table 4.8 below :

The table shows that 23 per cent of the respondent (leaders) attached greater importance to sons' education. Those leaders have strong conviction on popular Galo saying '*Nyijir ge ao em nyibo be*' which means daughters belong to the strangers. These leaders do not see any utility in sending the daughters to the schools. The leaders who prefer daughter's education were only 5 per cent, which is discouraging but equally important. But, the encouraging aspect of the table is that 72 per cent of the leaders do not have preference rather they pay equal importance to the education of both the sons and daughters. The overall analysis of the table reveals that the leaders pay slightly lesser importance to the girls' education but great majority of them do not discriminate between son and daughter. Hence, though not very significant, the table throws a light on changing perception of the leaders on the girls' education. The changed outlook is more eminent among the modern leaders compared to the traditional ones. This is displayed by the leader-wise break-up of the response because

Table 4.8. Distribution of the Respondents Showing Their Preference of Education to Their Children

	Traditional leaders				*Modern leaders*				
Response	*GAM*	*VE*	*PR*	*TL*	*PM*	*PL*	*CL*	*TL*	*G.TL*
Son	18	11	3	32	9	6	4	19	51
	(26)	(29)	(33)	(27)	(20)	(20)	(14)	(18)	(23)
Daughter	5	1	N	6	4	2	N	6	12
	(7)	(3)		(5)	(9)	(7)		(6)	(5)
Equally (both)	47	26	6	79	33	22	24	79	158
	(67)	(68)	(67)	(68)	(72)	(73)	(86)	(76)	(72)
Total	70	38	9	117	46	30	28	104	221
	(100)	(100)	(100)	(100)	(100)	(100)	(100)	(100)	(100)

percentage of the leaders who preferred son's education is larger among the traditional leaders (27 %). It was 26 per cent among *Gams*, 29 per cent among the village elders and 33 per cent among the priest whereas the modern leaders who preferred son's education was 18 per cent *i.e.* 20 per cent each among the Panchayat members and the party leaders and 14 per cent among the Church leader. The proportion of leaders who preferred daughter's education and who do not have preference is also proportionately higher among the modern leaders (6% and 76% respectively) when compared to the traditional leaders (5% and 68% respectively). Hence, the leader-wise break-up of the table confirms that the modern leaders are comparatively more liberal and progressive in their perception.

RIGHT TO INHERITANCE

The customary rules of the Galos do not recognize daughters' right to inheritance to immovable properties. The stray cases of daughter inheriting the paternal properties are the rarest of rare and it is usually circumstantial rather than a norm. Of course, the daughter has claim over mother's beads *(Tadok)* and it is usually given to her provided the later and her husband's family supply *Apong* and meat or fish to her parents at regular intervals or the parent take mithuns or cattle exceeding the traditional rate of bride price. Though the daughters are presented with traditional ornaments or necklace *(Adam Tadok)* at regular intervals throughout her lifetime, she cannot claim it as a matter of right especially over the landed properties. To know the leader's opinion on daughter's right of inheritance, they were asked, "Do you think the daughter should also be given equal rights of inheritance to landed properties?" Their response is presented in table 4.9 :

The table reveals the changing perceptions of the leaders regarding the status of women in the Galo society. Considering the rural background of the respondents, 33 per cent who favour daughters right to inheritance, is a very significant trend of changing perception. But majority (53%) of the leaders did not favour right to inheritance of the daughters. It seems that the message of gender equality

Table 4.9. Distribution of the Respondents Showing Their Opinion on Daughter's Right to Inherit Landed Properties

Response	*Traditional leaders*				*Modern leaders*				
	GAM	*VE*	*PR*	*TL*	*PM*	*PL*	*CL*	*TL*	*G.TL*
Yes	18	16	2	36	17	11	8	36	72
	(26)	(42)	(22)	(31)	(37)	(37)	(29)	(35)	(33)
No	46	16	3	65	24	16	12	52	117
	(66)	(42)	(33)	(56)	(52)	(53)	(43)	(50)	(53)
Don't know	6	6	4	16	5	3	8	16	32
	(9)	(16)	(44)	(14)	(11)	(10)	(29)	(15)	(14)
Total	70	38	9	117	46	30	28	104	221
	(100)	(100)	(100)	(100)	(100)	(100)	(100)	(100)	(100)

and women empowerment is yet to percolate down to the fabric of Galo society. The one-third seats reservation in the recently concluded Panchayat election was the first ever-formal occasion through which they came to know about the women empowerment. Otherwise, they were neither conscious nor concerned about the women empowerment. The 14 per cent of leaders did not have the idea about the daughter's right to inherit paternal properties. The leader-wise break-up of the response and comparative study reveals that the 'yes' percentage is proportionately higher among the modern leaders (35%) when compared to the traditional leaders (31%). The leader-wise break-up is 26 per cent among the *Gams*, 42 per cent among the village elders and 22 per cent among the priests but in case of modern leaders, it is 37 per cent each among the Panchayat and the party leaders and 29 per cent among the church leaders. But, conversely, the 'no' percentage is proportionately higher among the traditional leaders (56%) when compared to the 50 per cent of the modern leaders, but the difference is not so significant for meaningful generalization. Yet, overall analysis of the table reveals a perceptible change in the opinion of the leaders.

WIDOW REMARRIAGE

It is observed that there is no specific norm in Galo society to govern the issue of widow-remarriage. There are so many instances of widow going back to parent's home and remarry thereafter, but equally enormous is the instances where the widows themselves prefer to stay in deceased husband's family. It is also observed that sometimes, a widow is looked after by deceased's brother or sometimes, she goes back to her parent's home. Such decision is not governed by any specific norm, rather by factors like relative intimacy of the two families, wishes of the widow and number of the offsprings a widow has. The widow remarriage is an important issue not only in Galo society but in other societies as well. This issue needs to be considered with humane approach. To know the leaders' opinion about the widow remarriage in Galo society, they were asked, "Do you support/encourage widow remarriage?" Their response is given in table 4.10 below :

Table 4.10. Distribution of the Respondents Showing Their Opinion on Widow Remarriage

Response	*No. of Respondents*	*Percentage*
Yes	127	57
No	40	18
Can't say	54	24
Total	221	100

During the course of interview and discussions, it was revealed that 57 per cent of the leaders support the widow remarriage; only 18 per cent said 'no'. However, 24 per cent of the respondents were found to be confused and could not give clear verdict. The data reveals a significant breakthrough in the social outlook of the leaders. The traditional perception of bride as a commodity holds no more in the changing scenario. Only small minorities of leaders were opposed to the idea of widow remarriage. However, substantial proportions of leaders were found to be trapped between traditional ethos and modern sense of justice and equality. But, majority of the respondents were rational, humane and gender neutral in their opinion on this particular question. The leader-wise response is not reflected in the table, as the differences in the opinion of various types of leaders were not significant.

ROLE OF WOMEN IN *KEBA*

So far its composition and way of deliberation is concerned, the *Keba* is a democratic institution wherein all the members of the village can take part. However, it is observed that the active participation of women in the *Keba* is almost 'nil' though there is no such customary bar on their participation. One important reason is that Galo society is patriarchal and patrilineal and, therefore, the role of the male is always predominant in almost all spheres of life. Secondly, the females with their inherent household responsibilities find it inconvenient to attend the sittings of the *Keba*, which is a prolonged activity, sometimes sits for days together. The *Keba* is, thus, an all male affair. The women's role practically confines to private domains only.

Table 4.11. Distribution of the Respondents Showing Their Opinion on Role of Women in *Keba*

	Traditional leaders				*Modern leaders*				
Response	*GAM*	*VE*	*PR*	*TL*	*PM*	*PL*	*CL*	*TL*	*G.TL*
Yes	35 (50)	26 (68)	5 (56)	66 (56)	32 (70)	18 (60)	15 (54)	65 (62)	131 (59)
No	13 (19)	3 (8)	1 (11)	17 (15)	4 (9)	4 (13)	2 (7)	10 (10)	27 (12)
To some extent	22 (31)	9 (24)	3 (33)	34 (29)	10 (22)	8 (27)	11 (39)	29 (28)	63 (29)
Total	70 (100)	48 (100)	9 (100)	117 (100)	46 (100)	30 (100)	28 (100)	104 (100)	221 (100)

They do not play any significant role in community decision-making structure, though by her tact, efficiency and intelligence, she can get her decisions accepted by the *Keba*. "But even if rules, she never reigns"[8]. Thus, to know the leaders' perception on the role of women in the *Keba*, they were asked, "Do you think that women are also equally capable to take part in the *Keba*?" Their response is presented in table 4.11 below :

The table reveals that majority of the leaders felt women are also equally capable of taking part in the *Keba* deliberations. As we can see, 59 per cent of the respondents said 'yes' and the 'no' percentage is only 12 per cent. But, 29 per cent of the leaders had reservation over the capability of the women as decision-makers in the *Keba* and hence, said that women are capable to some extent only. Though, women practically do not participate in the corporate decision-making forum, it was found that majority of the leaders did not have biasness against the participation of women in *Keba*. The comparative analysis of their response reveals that the 'yes' percentage is higher among the modern leaders (62%) when compared to the traditional leaders (56%). The leader-wise break-up of the 'yes' percentage is 70 per cent among the Panchayat members, 60 per cent among the party leaders and 54 per cent among the church leaders, but in case of the traditional leaders, it is 50 per cent among the *Gam*, 68 per cent among the village elders and 56 per cent among the priests. But in case of 'no' percentage, the proportion of traditional leader (15%) is higher than that of the modern leaders (10%). The overall analysis of the table reveals that the emerging leaders are slightly more liberal towards the women's participation in the decision-making process of the traditional *Keba*.

APPOINTMENT OF WOMEN AS *GAM*

Since its inception, the office of the *Gam* is occupied by the male only because the government appoints only the male as *Gam* though there is no specific provisions in the law debarring the women from holding the post. Thus, to seek

8. Pandey, B.B., *Leadership Pattern in a Tribal Society*, Spectrum Publication, Guwahati & Delhi, 1991, p. 33.

Table 4.12. Distribution of the Respondents Showing Their Opinion on Appointment of Women as *Gam*

Response	*Traditional leaders*				*Modern leaders*				
	GAM	*VE*	*PR*	*TL*	*PM*	*PL*	*CL*	*TL*	*G.TL*
Yes	46	28	6	80	32	22	18	72	152
	(66)	(74)	(67)	(68)	(70)	(73)	(64)	(69)	(69)
No	19	7	2	28	8	6	6	20	48
	(27)	(18)	(22)	(24)	(17)	(20)	(22)	(19)	(22)
Can't say	5	3	1	9	6	2	4	12	21
	(7)	(8)	(11)	(8)	(13)	(7)	(14)	(12)	(9)
Total	70	38	9	117	46	30	28	104	221
	(100)	(100)	(100)	(100)	(100)	(100)	(100)	(100)	(100)

the opinion of the leaders on whether the women should also be appointed as *Gam*, they were asked, "Do you think that the women should also be appointed as *Gam*"? Their response is presented below in table 4.12 :

The table reveals that 69 per cent of the leaders wanted that the women too should be appointed as *Gam*. Thus, the majority of the respondent (leaders) recognized the equality of sex in holding the post of *Gam*. But 22 per cent of the leaders who said 'no' still subscribe to the traditional view that women cannot play a leading role in decision-making process in the village. 9 per cent of the leaders were found to be indecisive to respond the question or they were having some reservation on the question under consideration. The analysis reveals that the leaders, excepting few, did not have any biasness against the recruitment of women to the post of *Gam* but the government itself do not usually appoint a woman as *Gam*. That's why, we found only two women *Gams* in fifteen villages of our study area. The comparison of the pattern of response between the traditional and the modern leaders (68 per cent and 69 per cent respectively) do not show a significant shift in the opinion of the leaders on the question of appointment of women as *Gam* though there is little variation in the 'no' percentage *i.e.* 24 per cent and 19 per cent respectively among the traditional and the modern leaders. Further, data reveals that though the traditional leaders are usually considered as orthodox, but are quite progressive is nature, especially on the question of recruitment of women as *Gam*.

RESERVATION OF SEATS FOR WOMEN IN PRIs

Under the framework of the 73rd Constitution Amendment Act, the one-third of the seats in Panchayat bodies is being reserved for the women for the first time in India. This was a new message for the rural population. Though the Galo society accords high status to the women in the society, the women never enjoyed such status in the corporate decision-making forum. Thus, the message of reservation was received with mixed response in the Galo society. Thus, to know leaders' opinion on the question, they were asked, "Do you favour the reservation of seats for women in

Table 4.13. Distribution of the Respondents Showing Their Opinion on Reservation of Seats for Women in the Panchayat Bodies

Response	*Traditional leaders*				*Modern leaders*				
	GAM	*VE*	*PR*	*TL*	*PM*	*PL*	*CL*	*TL*	*G.TL*
Yes	37	26	3	66	32	18	17	67	133
	(53)	(68)	(33)	(56)	(70)	(60)	(61)	(64)	(60)
No	24	9	3	36	12	12	7	31	67
	(34)	(24)	(33)	(31)	(26)	(40)	(25)	(30)	(30)
Don't know	9	3	3	15	2	N	4	6	21
	(13)	(8)	(33)	(13)	(4)		(14)	(6)	(10)
Total	70	38	9	117	46	30	28	104	221
	(100)	(100)	(99)	(100)	(100)	(100)	(100)	(100)	(100)

Panchayat bodies?" Their response is presented in table 4.13 .

Though women reservation is a new concept for the villagers, the majority (60%) of the leaders liked the reservation of seats for women in the Panchayat bodies. Given the patriarchal nature of the society and restricted role of the women in the traditional decision-making process, the table reveals significant positive change in the perception of the leaders. Only 30 per cent of the respondents dislike the idea of women reservation in Panchayat bodies and 10 per cent of the leaders could not give clear opinion on the question. The comparative study of the pattern of the response reveals that the 'yes' percentage is higher among the modern leaders (64%) when compared to the traditional leaders (56%), but the respondents who negatively replied constitute of 31 per cent and 30 per cent respectively. The leader-wise 'yes' percentage is 53 per cent among the *Gam*, 68 per cent among the village elders and 33 per cent among the priests but in case of modern leaders, it is 70 per cent among the Panchayat members, 60 per cent among the party leaders and 61 per cent among the Church leaders. It was observed that the leaders who said 'no' did not like the women reservation because some male aspirants could not file the nomination from the reserved seats and some other said that there will be problem in managing household activities and hence, tension within family may ensue. Thus, it was noticed that their reasons for disapproval of the women reservation was personal and contextual only and at times driven by selfish aspirations.

STATE OF THE *KEBA*

Apart from the study of the leaders' opinion and perception on some socio-cultural issues, few more questions regarding the contemporary state of the *Keba* and its leadership was put to them. It is observed that the hold of the traditional leaders like *Gams* on society has reduced. The traditional leaders of the *Keba* are no more popular and influential in the village as they used to be. Consequently, people's faith on village *Keba* is gradually eroding. The analysis of the leaders' response to the following questions would testify our observation.

Table 4.14

	Traditional leaders				Modern leaders				
Responses	*GAM*	*VE*	*PR*	*TL*	*PM*	*PL*	*CL*	*TL*	*G.TL*
Gam	39	16	4	59	15	9	9	33	92
	(56)	(42)	(44)	(50)	(33)	(30)	(32)	(32)	(42)
Pan. Member	12	4	N	16	14	4	4	22	38
	(17)	(11)		(14)	(30)	(13)	(14)	(21)	(17)
Party leader	16	11	4	31	14	12	10	36	67
	(23)	(29)	(44)	(26)	(30)	(40)	(36)	(35)	(30)
Rich man	3	7	1	11	4	8	5	17	28
	(4)	(18)	(11)	(9)	(9)	(27)	(18)	(16)	(13)

Note : Total is not shown as some respondents gave more than one response. So, total exceeds the actual number of respondents.

Question : "Who, do you think, is more popular as leader in the village at present?" The response is given in table 4.14.

As table 3.14 reveals, 42 per cent of the leaders consider *Gam* as a more popular leader than other leaders. It is followed by party leaders (30%), Panchayat leaders (17%) and rich-man (13%). It is evident that though *Gams* score the highest, their position as leader has significantly diminished in the eye of the leaders themselves. The party leaders are gaining popularity at the cost of the *Gams'* status. It was opined by many respondents that one cannot be a leader of the panchayat bodies without being an active party worker. The rich people have their own sphere of influence through their money power. The leader-wise break-up of the response reveals that compared to modern leaders (32%), greater proportion (50%) of traditional leaders consider *Gam* as more popular leader, it is 56 per cent among the *Gam*, 42 per cent among the village elder and 44 per cent among the priest but in case of the modern leaders, it is 33 per cent among the panchayat members, 30 per cent among the party leaders and 32 per cent among the church leaders. But the leader who considers panchayat member or party leader or rich-man as more popular leader is proportionately higher among the modern leaders. The proportion of respondents who considered panchayat member as more popular leader constituted 14 per cent of the traditional leaders and 21 per cent of the modern leaders, the highest proportion being the panchayat members themselves (30%). Those who considered party leader as more popular leader constituted of 26 per cent of the traditional leaders and 35 per cent of the modern leaders, the highest proportion being the party leaders themselves (40%) and the priest (44%) and those who said rich-man was 9 per cent among the traditional leaders and 16 per cent among the modern leaders. Thus, there is the tendency on the part of different types of leaders to assert their own status.

Question : "Who, do you think, has greater influence in the society/village at present?" The response are given in the table 4.15.

Table 4.15

Responses	*Traditional leaders*				*Modern leaders*				
	GAM	*VE*	*PR*	*TL*	*PM*	*PL*	*CL*	*TL*	*G.TL*
Gam	46	18	3	67	17	8	14	39	106
	(66)	(47)	(33)	(57)	(37)	(27)	(50)	(37)	(48)
Panchayat Member	9	6	N	15	15	7	6	28	42
	(13)	(16)		(13)	(33)	(23)	(21)	(27)	(19)
Party Leader	10	10	3	23	12	13	8	33	56
	(14)	(26)	(33)	(20)	(26)	(43)	(29)	(32)	(25)
Priest	5	4	3	12	2	2	N	4	17
	(7)	(11)	(33)	(10)	(4)	(7)		(4)	(8)
Total	70	38	9	117	46	30	28	104	221
	(100)	(100)	(99)	(100)	(100)	(100)	(100)	(100)	(100)

The table reveals that in spite of changing power structure, the *Gam* remains the most influential among different types of leaders within the village. 48 per cent of the leaders conceded that *Gam* has greater influence in the village affairs. It is followed by party leaders (25%), panchayat members (19%) and priest (8%) only. In this analysis also, there is indication that the party leaders are becoming more powerful because of their contact and exposure to the outside world and higher-level leaders at the district and state level. The influence of the priest is largely confined to the local areas and with sacred activities only. The comparative analysis of the response of both the traditional and modern leaders reveals that proportionately greater percentage of traditional leaders named themselves as more influential. Whereas, in the same way, greater percentage of the modern leaders termed themselves as more influential. The proportion of the respondent leaders who consider *Gam* as more influential constituted of 57 per cent of the traditional leaders and 37 per cent of the modern leaders—the highest proportion being the *Gam* (66%). Those who named Panchayat members were 13 per cent among the traditional leaders and 27 per cent among the modern leaders—the highest proportion being the Panchayat members (33%) and those who consider party leaders as more influential is also proportionately higher among the modern leaders (32%) when compared to the traditional leaders (20%)—the highest proportion being the party leaders themselves (43%). Those who named priest as influential was but higher among the traditional leaders (10%) than the modern leaders (4%)—the highest proportion being the priest (33%). In this study also, the tendency among each type of leaders to assert their respective position and status could be clearly observed. The broad conclusion of this table is that the influence of the *Gam* has reduced to a great extent and it is conceded by the 44 per cent of the respondent *Gams* themselves. This is a significant trend of change in the grassroots leadership phenomenon.

Question : "Do you think that introduction of panchayat has undermined the status of *Gam*?" Their response is presented in table 4.16.

Table 4.16

	Traditional leaders				*Modern leaders*				
Responses	*GAM*	*VE*	*PR*	*TL*	*PM*	*PL*	*CL*	*TL*	*G.TL*
Yes	26 (37)	11 (29)	3 (33)	40 (34)	15 (33)	8 (26)	9 (32)	32 (31)	73 (33)
No	25 (36)	15 (39)	3 (33)	43 (37)	18 (39)	11 (37)	15 (54)	44 (42)	87 (39)
To some extent	19 (27)	12 (32)	3 (33)	34 (29)	13 (28)	11 (37)	4 (14)	28 (27)	62 (28)
Total	70 (100)	38 (100)	9 (99)	117 (100)	46 (100)	30 (100)	28 (100)	104 (100)	221 (100)

The table reveals that 33 per cent of the leaders clearly said that introduction of panchayat have undermined the status of *Gam*. Those who negatively responded are only 39 per cent. 28 per cent of the respondents agreed that introduction of panchayat has undermined the status of *Gam* to some extent only. Thus, analysis of the table reveals that majority of the leaders conceded openly or tacitly that panchayat has undermined the status of *Gam*. The table further reveals that the 'Yes' percentage is slightly higher among the traditional leaders (34%) when compared to the modern leaders (31%). The proportion of respondents who said "to some extent" is also slightly higher among the traditional leaders (29%) than the modern leaders (27%). From this analysis, we can assume that the traditional leaders are aware of their diminishing status in the society. The striking feature of the table is that 'Yes' percentage is highest among the *Gam*, which meant that the *Gams* themselves are fully aware of the changing power structure in the village.

Question : "Do you think that the common people have still good faith on *Keba*?" Their response is given in table 4.17.

The 76 per cent of the leaders opined that common people have still good faith on *Keba*. The 'No' percentage is only 8 per cent. 18 per cent of them think that peoples' faith on *Keba* is loosing and their faith is situational only. Thus, we can assume through this analysis that the relevance and sanctity of the *Keba* is still high in the Galo society, but at the same time we cannot ignore the declining trend of *Keba* as traditional village authority. The comparison of the pattern of response reveals that greater proportion (79%) of the traditional leaders considered that common people have still good faith on *Keba*, when compared to the modern leaders (72%). Those who said 'No' was 6 per cent and 7 per cent respectively among the traditional and the modern leaders, and those who said 'to some extent' was 15 per cent and 2 per cent respectively. Thus, we can assume that the traditional leaders have relatively greater degree of respect for the *Keba* or they are less able to perceive the loosing

Table 4.17

Responses	Traditional leaders				Modern leaders				
	GAM	*VE*	*PR*	*TL*	*PM*	*PL*	*CL*	*TL*	*G.TL*
Yes	59	27	6	92	33	24	18	75	167
	(84)	(71)	(67)	(79)	(72)	(80)	(64)	(72)	(76)
No	3	2	2	7	2	3	2	7	14
	(4)	(5)	(22)	(6)	(4)	(10)	(7)	(7)	(8)
To some extent	8	9	1	18	11	3	8	22	40
	(12)	(24)	(11)	(15)	(24)	(10)	(29)	(21)	(18)
Total	70	38	9	117	46	30	28	104	221
	(99)	(100)	(100)	(100)	(100)	(100)	(100)	(100)	(100)

faith of the people on *Keba* when compared to the modern leaders. But the variations in the response of different types of leaders are marginally low and do not indicate any important shift.

Question : "Which of the following factor is most important for leadership at grassroots level? Their response is given in table 4.18.

The analysis of the above table reveals a major shift in the leadership pattern in terms of its determinants because educational background and party support are found to be important determinants, which were never relevant for leadership in the traditional Galo society. Education, as stated, emerges as the most important factor for leadership (46%). Integrity and honesty, a general tribal trait, is relegated to secondary position as only 30 per cent of the respondents consider it as an important factor. Wisdom and knowledge about tradition, which was a strong basis of tribal leadership, is no more an important factor as only 17 per cent of the leaders consider it as important determinants of leadership. The family background and economic status are also an important aspect of leadership (11%) and (12%) respectively. The overview of the table shows that new variables like education and party support are becoming more crucial factors of leadership and traditional determinants like wisdom and knowledge about tradition, family status and integrity-honesty are loosing its significance. The table further reveals that 51 per cent of the traditional leaders said that educational background is the most important determinants of leadership but it is only 40 per cent among the modern leaders. Accordingly, the traditional leaders attach, proportionately, greater degree of importance to the educational attainment than the modern leaders. Those who considered 'family background' and 'economic status' as determinants of leadership constituted 9 per cent each among traditional leaders but 12 per cent and 16 per cent respectively among the modern leader. 19 per cent of the traditional leaders and 15 per cent of the modern leaders preferred the 'knowledge about tradition' as an important determinant. 'Party support'

Table 4.18

	Traditional leaders				Modern leaders				
Responses	*GAM*	*VE*	*PR*	*TL*	*PM*	*PL*	*CL*	*TL*	*G.TL*
Education	31 (44)	25 (66)	4 (44)	60 (51)	15 (36)	9 (30)	18 (64)	42 (40)	102 (46)
Family background	8 (11)	1 (3)	2 (22)	11 (9)	7 (15)	1 (3)	5 (18)	13 (12)	24 (11)
Economic status	5 (7)	4 (11)	1 (11)	10 (9)	10 (22)	4 (13)	3 (11)	17 (16)	27 (12)
Knowledge about tradition	13 (9)	8 (21)	1 (11)	22 (19)	8 (17)	6 (20)	2 (7)	16 (15)	38 (17)
Party support	7 (10)	7 (18)	1 (11)	15 (13)	5 (11)	8 (27)	4 (14)	17 (16)	32 (14)
Integrity-honesty	19 (67)	11 (29)	3 (33)	33 (28)	13 (28)	12 (40)	8 (29)	33 (32)	66 (30)

Note : Total is not shown as many respondents choose more than one response. So, total exceeds the actual number of respondents.

constituted 13 per cent among traditional leaders and 16 per cent among the modern leaders. Those who preferred 'integrity and honesty' as determinants of leadership were 28 per cent among the traditional leaders and 32 per cent among the modern leaders. Thus, it is observed that the difference in percentage of the respondents does not reveal a significant trend in the leader-wise pattern of response.

SUMMARY

The above study reveals that there has been considerable change in the attitudes and perceptions of the leaders. Their opinion on some important customary practices and other social issues like inter-tribal marriage, status and role of women, marriage celebration *(Togu)*, social taboos, etc., reflects a positive change in the attitude and perceptions of the leaders. Their opinion on bride price, inheritance to paternal properties, widow remarriage, role of women in *Keba*, women reservation, etc. shows that the women are not neglected in the Galo society. But, on certain issues like inheritance, education, and sex of the child, the leaders maintained relatively rigid stand in favour of the male child. However, the study of the leaders' opinion on some of the important issues like *Nyame Ginam*, bride-price, existing social taboos, inheritance, etc. shows that it is not easy to give up the customary practices in spite of the changing social environment. Further our analysis revealed that the modern leaders were comparatively more progressive in their outlook than the traditional leaders. The analysis of the leaders' response to the questions regarding the present state of *Keba* and its leadership reveals that the popularity and influence of the traditional leaders especially the *Gams* has decreased to some extent and consequently the people's faith on *Keba* is also diminishing.

5

Changing Pattern of Leadership and Decision-Making Process

Decision-making is one of the important functional aspects of leadership. It exhibits the nature of power structure and reflects the political awakening of the participants. The decision-making involves 'conscious choice or selection of behaviour alternative from among a group or two or more behaviour alternatives'[1]. In a political system, decision-making involves a dialectical functioning of the forces of conflict, competition, adjustment and cohesion. It also involves 'an aspect of power structure that is who influences whose acts in what ways'[2]. The decisions may be broadly categorized as consensus, majority and arbitrary decisions and it depends on the type of group in which a decision is taken. The authoritarian group may take an arbitrary decision without considering the wishes of the general population but the democratic groups are likely to take into account the wishes of common people also whereas consensus decision-making is considered as a common practice in the smaller groups where all the members' opinion is sought and incorporated.

The decision-making process in the traditional village community is different from that of the other organized groups and organizations. Decision-makers in formal

---

1. Verma, B.M., *Rural Leadership in a Welfare Society*, Mittal Publication, New Delhi, 1994, p. 90.
2. Mishra, S.M., *Political Socialization in Rural India*, Inter-India Publication, Delhi, 1989, p. 128.

organizations act under some influence specified by the rules, norms and expectations of the larger group to which they belong and in which they operate[3]. They usually follow a set pattern of decision-making method. Since organization is basically arranged in a hierarchy, centralization of decision-making power is an important dimension. But in rural or village community, 'the decision makers are often influenced by particularistic factors such as institutionalized obligation of friendship, kinship, caste, other primary regional loyalties and loyalties to political parties. Very often, the decisions tended to be person-oriented rather than problem-oriented'[4]. Sometimes, decision-making depends on individual personality of the decision-maker, though relation between 'personality' and decision-making, historically of interest to political analysts but long confined to anecdotes and speculation, still awaits sustained systematic study[5]. There has been perceptible change in the traditional political set up and its decision-making process due to the rapid process of modernization and introduction of the devolution of power in the villages. In the changed political set-up, the decision-making process, at least in principle, aims at 'combining the popular elements with the ingredients of expertise in the final decisional product'[6].

METHODS OF DECISION-MAKING

The traditional Galo society has slightly different method of decision-making in the *Keba*. Due to the absence of social stratification and institutionalized hereditary leadership (headship) in the village and the lack of decision—making dynamism, the Galo *Keba* takes a decision by consensus. "Decisions of the *Kebang* are supposed to come from the

3. See *Encyclopedia of the Social Science,* Vol. 3 & 4 (ed.) David L. Sills, Macmillan Company, New York, 1968, pp. 59-60.
4. Mishra, S.N., *Political Socialization in Rural India,* Inter-India Publication, Delhi, 1980, p. 127.
5. See *Encyclopedia of the Social Science,* Vol. 3 & 4 (ed.) David L. Silla, Macmillan Company, New York, 1968.
6. Mishra, S.N., *Political Socialization in Rural India,* Inter-India Publication, Delhi, 1980, p. 126.

people. The *Gams* or headmen help only to enforce it"[7]. The traditional Galo *Keba* had no *Gam* or headmen as such, but the institution of *Gam* is an official innovation super-imposed on the traditional authority structure. He is influential in the village, not because of any hereditary factor, but because of his personal skill and commitment to serve the society coupled with official sanction to his authority. Further, the Galo *Keba* does not have separate body to deal with civil, criminal and developmental issues separately, rather, decision on all the issues are taken by the same people in the village. Hence, the leaders play an overlapping role in decision-making process. But the role of the traditional *Keba* is more prominent in taking a decision regarding the matters of judicial nature, though other matters are also taken up. 'The aim of the *Kebang* is to make the parties agree to a compromise in the court and not to pass a judgement to be enforced'[8] and deliberations have to continue till all including the disputants come to a consensus. Thus, decision by consensus was the usual method of decision-making in the traditional Galo society. But, in our study, it was assumed that with the changes in the traditional political environment, there has been considerable change in the methods of decision making too. With the changing perception of the people and increasing knowledge of modern system of justice, the decision by consensus is becoming difficult to arrive at. Collectivism and cohesiveness was the basic characteristics of the rural areas but the present trends show a general degeneration of traditional authority and corporate living. The traditional customs stand modified and old relationships are strained, hence decisions are no more guided by traditional spirit of simplicity and truthfulness. Thus, the leaders were asked, "How decisions are usually arrived at the village *Keba*?"

The table 5.1 reveals that the leaders usually adopt the democratic method of decision-making but the traditional method of decision-making by consensus is on declining

7. Elwin, Verrier, *Democracy in NEFA* (reprint), Directorate of Research, Govt. of Arunachal Pradesh, Itanagar, 1988, p. 111.

8. Nyori, Tai, *History and Culture of the Adis*, Omsons Publication, New Delhi, 1993, p. 135.

Table 5.1. Distribution of the Respondents Showing Their Methods of Decision-Making

Response	*Traditional leaders*				*Modern leaders*				
	GAM	*VE*	*PR*	*TL*	*PM*	*PL*	*CL*	*TL*	*G. TL*
Consensus	24	13	2	39	20	6	8	34	73
	(34)	(34)	(22)	(33)	(43)	(20)	(29)	(33)	(33)
Majority	39	24	6	69	23	16	15	54	123
	(56)	(63)	(67)	(59)	(50)	(53)	(54)	(52)	(56)
Arbitrarily by	7	1	1	9	3	8	5	16	25
Leaders	(10)	(3)	(11)	(8)	(7)	(27)	(18)	(15)	(11)
Total	70	38	9	117	46	30	28	104	221
	(100)	(100)	(100)	(100)	(100)	(100)	(100)	(100)	(100)

trend. The leaders who said that decisions are taken by consensus methods constitute only 33 per cent of the total respondents whereas those who said 'majority' constitute 56 per cent of the total respondents. Thus, majority of the leaders conceded that the decisions are usually arrived at by majority method. Further, 11 per cent of the respondent leaders said that the decision at village *Keba* is arbitrarily taken by the leaders, hence, we can assume that some leaders are adopting an undemocratic method of decision-making. The comparative study of the table reveals that both the traditional leaders and modern leaders have almost similar view on the consensus method of decision-making *i.e.* 33 per cent each, but the respondents who said 'majority' is proportionately higher among the traditional leaders (59%) when compared to the modern leaders (52%). The leader-wise break-up of the respondents who said, 'consensus' was 56 per cent among the *Gams*, 63 per cent among the village elders and 67 per cent among the priests but in case of modern leaders, it was 50 per cent among the Panchayat members, 53 per cent among the party leaders and 54 per cent among the church leaders. But the respondents who said that decisions are taken arbitrarily by the leaders is proportionately higher among the modern leaders (15%) in comparison to the traditional leaders (8%). The leader-wise break-up was 7 per cent among the Panchayat members, 27 per cent among party leaders and 18 per cent among the church leaders but in case of the traditional leaders, it is 10 per cent among the *Gams*, 3 per cent among the village elders and 11 per cent among the priests. Thus, it is interesting to note that in terms of decision-making, the so-called modern leaders who represent the democratic institutions of statutory Panchayats and the parties are less democratic than the traditional leaders. In the course of our interview, it was confessed by many leaders, basically the Panchayat and party leaders that they had to take arbitrary decisions at times, to follow the dictate of the party in power and the higher level leaders like Zilla Parishad Members and Members of Legislative Assembly. Though, at times overlapping, the traditional leaders and modern leaders have separate role in the decision-making process.

However, the difference is very thin. The decisions on the issues of judicial nature are usually taken in the *Keba* under the guidance of the traditional leaders like *Gams* and the village elders and hence, there is greater scope for discussion and deliberation in the village *Keba,* which paves the way for consensus or majority decisions. But, in developmental issues in which the role of the modern leaders like Panchayat members and party leaders are more prominent, their decisions are often guided by the party interest and the dictates of the so-called high command, and hence, the decisions sometime become arbitrary and undemocratic because the diverse and conflicting interests of political parties, influential people, official formalities etc. are to be accommodated while taking a decision on developmental issues. It is usually observed in the villages that decisions regarding the selection of beneficiaries of various rural development programmes, awarding of government contract works, selection of site for irrigation and flood control projects etc. are not necessarily taken on the merit of the cases. But such decisions are usually determined by the party interest, personal influence and personal relationship of a person with higher-level leaders and the officers. Thus, decisions, sometimes, tended to be arbitrary and undemocratic.

EXECUTION OF *KEBA* DECISION

Since *Keba* is an informal traditional institution, there is no separate organ for legislation and execution of its decisions. The *Keba* is a total corporate body, which performs all the functions including deliberation, execution and the arbitration. There is scope for universal participation of men in decision-making process in the *Keba.* The execution of *Keba* decision is, therefore, spontaneous because everyone is, in principle, party to the decisions. "Decisions of the *Kebang* are supposed to come from the people. The *Gams* or headmen help only enforce it. The injunctions are obeyed to the letter, for these people are respectful of their ancient customs and traditional laws"[9]. Traditionally, as *Keba*

9. Elwin, Verrier, *Democracy in NEFA* (reprint), Directorate of Research, Govt. of Arunachal Pradesh, Itanagar, 1988, pp. 111-112.

upholds the values of impartiality and neutrality in reaching at decisions, which are usually democratically decided through the mass participation, the instances of disobedience are very rare. Usually, due to the very nature of corporate life, seldom any person penalized by the *Keba* resort to disobedience. Nevertheless, due to various influences, these days, instances of defiant attitude on the part of the party who is being penalized cannot be overruled. The traditional practice was that in case of disobedience to the *Keba* decision by an individual, the *Keba* depute few individuals to snatch some household article of daily use from disobedient person. This was known as '*Lako*' in Galo terminology. Such snatched article is returned to the owner only when the disobedient person beg apology and subscribe to the *Keba* decision. Otherwise, the article is kept as *Keba* property or sold off in a cheaper rate. 'This was an important deterrent punishment because pride and self-esteem is a powerful psychological force in tribal society; it is the reason for the great feast on which men spends the savings of many years. The public condemnation and such loss of face is more effective deterrent punishment than going to jail or actual cost of the article'[10]. The customary system of '*Lako*' was a popular pressure tactics adopted not by individual leader but by the *Keba* as a whole, but such method is rarely resorted to at present. On some instances, the influential close relative convinces the disobedient individual to obey the *Keba* decision especially in the cases of imposition of fines and compensations. Thus, the respondents were asked, "What steps do you generally take in the village to execute *Keba* decisions?"

The analysis of the table 4.2 reveals that 7 per cent of the respondent leaders use pressure tactics to execute the *Keba* decision but majority (51%) of the respondent leaders use the democratic method of persuasion for the same. The 16 per cent of them confessed that they take the help of the influential people to execute the *Keba* decision, whereas a considerable proportion (27%) of leaders said that they do

10. See 'Tribal Idea of the Guilt and Punishment' in *Democracy in NEFA* (reprint) by Verrier Elwin, Directorate of Research, Govt. of Arunachal Pradesh, Itanagar, 1988.

Table 5.2. Distribution of the Respondents Showing Their Method of Execution of *Keba* Decisions

	Traditional leaders				*Modern leaders*				
Response	*GAM*	*VE*	*PR*	*TL*	*PM*	*PL*	*CL*	*TL*	*G. TL*
Pressure	4 (6)	N	1 (11)	5 (4)	6 (13)	3 (10)	2 (7)	11 (11)	16 (7)
Persuasion	39 (56)	25 (66)	1 (11)	65 (56)	18 (39)	16 (53)	13 (46)	47 (45)	112 (51)
Approach through influential people	9 (13)	7 (18)	3 (33)	19 (16)	9 (20)	6 (20)	1 (4)	16 (15)	35 (16)
Not specific	18 (26)	6 (16)	4 (45)	28 (44)	13 (28)	5 (17)	12 (43)	30 (29)	58 (26)
Total	70 (100)	38 (100)	9 (100)	117 (100)	46 (100)	30 (100)	28 (100)	104 (100)	221 (100)

not employ any specific method. The leader-wise break-up of their response shows that the percentage of leaders who employ pressure tactic is proportionately higher among the modern leaders (11%) when compared to the traditional leaders (4%). The leader-wise break-up was 13 per cent among the Panchayat members, 10 per cent among the party leaders and 7 per cent among the church leader but in case of traditional leaders who employ pressure tactics were 6 per cent among the *Gams*, 11 per cent among the priests and no village elders employ pressure methods. The percentage of the leaders who use persuasion method was proportionately higher among the traditional leaders (56%) when compared to the modern leaders (45%). The leader-wise break-up was 56 per cent among the *Gams*, 66 per cent among the village elders and 11 per cent among the priest but in case of the modern leaders, it was 39 per cent among the Panchayat members, 53 per cent among the party leaders and 46 per cent among the church leaders. The proportion of the respondents who take the help of the influential people to execute the *Keba* decision was almost similar between the traditional leaders (16%) and the modern leaders (15%). And, those who do not employ specific method was 24 per cent among the traditional leaders and 29 per cent among the modern leaders. Thus, in comparison, the greater proportion of respondent among the modern leaders use undemocratic method such as pressure and influence through influential people to execute the *Keba* decision in the village. This is so because, the decision of the modern leaders specially regarding the developmental issues is more often guided by the party interest and dictates of the higher-level political leaders. The traditional village *Keba* is less exposed to the political interference though we cannot ignore the same.

SANCTITY OF THE *KEBA* DECISION

Disobedience of village *Keba* decision is not uncommon at present. It is usually observed that there have been many instances of *Keba* decision being challenged and appealed for arbitration at the formal judiciary. Taking this phenomenon into account, the respondents were asked, "Do

Table 5.3. Distribution of the Respondents Showing Their Perception on Sanctity of the *Keba* Decision

Response	*Traditional leaders*				*Modern leaders*				
	GAM	*VE*	*PR*	*TL*	*PM*	*PL*	*CL*	*TL*	*G.TL*
Yes	21	13	1	35	7	12	7	26	61
	(30)	(34)	(12)	(30)	(15)	(40)	(25)	(25)	(28)
No	27	13	4	44	22	9	10	41	85
	(39)	(34)	(44)	(38)	(48)	(30)	(36)	(39)	(38)
To some extent	22	12	4	38	17	9	11	37	75
	(31)	(32)	(44)	(32)	(37)	(30)	(39)	(36)	(34)
Total	70	38	9	117	46	30	28	104	221
	(100)	(100)	(100)	(100)	(100)	(100)	(100)	(100)	(100)

you think that people have tendency to disobey *Keba* decisions nowadays?" Responses are given in table 5.3.

The close analysis of their response reveals that all the people no longer abide by the decisions of the *Keba* in all the cases. *Keba* decisions are sometime challenged which indicates the deteriorating trend of the traditional authority. 28 per cent of the leaders conceded that there is a growing tendency to disobey the *Keba* decisions by the people. 'No' percentage is only 38 per cent but significantly 34 per cent of the respondents said that though there are instances of disobedience to *Keba* decision, such disobedience is not regular rather it is occasional and casual. Thus, opinion of the leaders reflected in table 1.27 reveals that the status of *Keba* as authoritative decision-making body has diminished to certain extent, which is indicative of the declining legitimacy of the traditional leaders like *Gam* and village elders. The comparative pattern of response shows that the 'Yes' percentage is slightly higher among the traditional leaders (30%) when compared to the modern leaders (25%), but those who said 'to some extent' is slightly higher among the modern leaders (36%) when compared to the traditional leaders (32%). The 'No' percentage is 38 per cent and 39 per cent respectively. Hence, the leader-wise pattern of response does not reveal significant shift and the proportion of difference in the percentage of response is too narrow to make a meaningful analysis.

METHOD OF INFLUENCE

At the present juncture, the political manoeuvering is an important tactic to garner the support of the people in the villages. It is observed that the common people usually do not want to earn the disfavour of the higher-level political leader like M.L.A. Under such circumstances, the leaders may employ political pressure in form of threat and deception to get loyalty of the general people. Besides, the leaders may appeal to the sentiments of family and clan relationship, because such relationship.is strictly maintained in the traditional Galo society. It was assumed that the analysis of methods adopted by the leaders to influence the people is necessary to understand the leaders' behaviour in the

Table 5.4. Distribution of the Respondents Showing Their Method of Influence

	Traditional leaders				*Modern leaders*				
Response	*GAM*	*VE*	*PR*	*TL*	*PM*	*PL*	*CL*	*TL*	*G. TL*
Political pressure	4 (6)	3 (8)	1 (11)	8 (7)	6 (13)	2 (7)	3 (11)	11 (11)	19 (9)
Family-clan pressure	3 (4)	2 (5)	N	5 (4)	3 (7)	4 (13)	4 (14)	11 (11)	16 (7)
Persuasion convincing	63 (90)	33 (87)	8 (89)	104 (89)	37 (80)	24 (80)	21 (75)	82 (78)	186 (84)
Total	70 (100)	38 (100)	9 (100)	117 (100)	46 (100)	30 (100)	28 (100)	104 (100)	221 (100)

decision-making situation. It will also reflect the role of politics and other primordial factors like family and clan relationship in the decision-making process, thereby, throw a light on the nature of decision-making in the village *Keba*. Taking these into consideration, we asked, "What methods do you generally adopt to get majority support of your viewpoint in the village?"

The analysis of the above table indicates that the great majority (84%) of the respondent leaders use democratic method of 'persuasion and convincing' to get support of their viewpoints in the village. But, 9 per cent of the leaders were found to be using the party politics as tools to influence the people. And 7 per cent of the total respondent leaders preferred to get support of the people by appealing to the sentiment of family and clan relationship. The overall picture of the table indicates that though the leaders are democratic in terms of the method of influence, some leaders adopt the undemocratic and divisive method of influence in the village. The leader-wise break-up of the same table shows that the proportion of leaders who adopt undemocratic methods like political pressure and family-clan pressure is comparatively higher among the modern leaders than the traditional leaders. The proportion of the respondents who employ political pressure constituted 7 per cent among the traditional leaders and 11 per cent among the modern leaders. And those who employ family-clan pressure were 4 per cent among the traditional leaders and 11 per cent among the modern leaders. The leader-wise percentage of the respondents who employ political pressure as means of influence constitutes, among the traditional leaders, 6 per cent of *Gams*, 8 per cent of the village elders and 11 per cent of the priests, whereas in case of the modern leaders, it is 13 per cent among the Panchayat member, 7 per cent among the party leaders and 11 per cent among the church leaders. Further, the leader-wise break-up who employ family and clan pressure are 4 per cent among the *Gams*, 5 per cent among the village elders and no priest adopt such means of influence but in case of modern leaders who employ family-clan pressure are 7 per cent among the Panchayat member, 13 per cent among the party leaders and 14 per cent among the church leaders. Hence, the percentage of leaders who adopt democratic methods of persuasion and convincing is proportionately higher among the traditional leaders (89%) when compared to the modern leaders (78%)—it is 90 per cent among the *Gams*, 87 per cent among the village elders and 89 per cent among the priests. At the same time, in case of the modern leaders, it is 80 per cent each amongst the Panchayat members and the party leaders, and 75 per cent among the church leaders. Thus, it is interesting to note that proportionately greater percentage of the traditional leaders adopt democratic means of influence when compared to the modern leaders. Equally, when it comes to the application of methods of influence, the traditional leaders are comparatively more democratic in their approach.

ROLE OF MONEY AND POWER

It is assumed in our study that money and power play a significant role in the process of arbitration in the village *Keba*. Here, power implies wealth, status, background and linkage of a person. Taking this as the background, the respondents were asked, "Do you think that money and power play a role in settling a dispute? The response is given in the table 5.5.

The tribal mode of justice is always quick, simple and free of cost, but leaders' opinion as reflected in the above table reveals that justice is no more simple, quick and free of cost as it used to be in traditional Galo society. 55 per cent of the leaders conceded that money and power play a role in settling a dispute and 29 per cent of them too tacitly recognized the role of money and power in settling a dispute occasionally. The 'No' percentage is sadly low *i.e.* 16 per cent only. The table further shows that those who said 'Yes' is proportionately higher among the modern leaders (59%) when compared to traditional leaders (52%), but those who said 'to some extent' is higher (32%) among the traditional leaders in comparison to the 26 per cent of modern leaders. So, comparative analysis does not show a definite shift in the pattern of response among the traditional and modern leaders.

Table 5.5. Distribution of the Respondents as Per Their Opinion on Role of Money and Power

	Traditional leaders				*Modern leaders*				
Responses	*GAM*	*VE*	*PR*	*TL*	*PM*	*PL*	*CL*	*TL*	*G.TL*
Yes	29 (41)	27 (71)	5 (56)	61 (52)	23 (60)	18 (60)	20 (72)	61 (59)	122 (55)
No	14 (20)	5 (13)	N	19 (16)	6 (13)	6 (20)	4 (14)	16 (15)	35 (16)
To some extent	27 (39)	6 (16)	4 (44)	37 (32)	17 (37)	6 (20)	4 (14)	27 (26)	64 (29)
Total	70 (100)	36 (100)	9 (100)	117 (100)	46 (100)	30 (100)	28 (100)	104 (100)	221 (100)

INFLUENCE OF PARTY POLITICS

Social harmony and cohesion in the village have been distorted to a great extent, among other factors, by the emergence of party politics in the village. The division of village population on party lines is not an uncommon phenomenon in the present context. There have been instances of organization of separate feast or picnic by the supporter of different political parties within the same village. The sense of unity and cooperation in the village is being slowly replaced by jealousy, envy, division and internal competition. The village folk are no more honest and truthful as they used to be. The construction of a dwelling house is a community affair in the Galo society but there are instances that people loyal to one party refuse to participate in the house construction of the other belonging to another party. Hence, it was assumed in our study that since party politics has penetrated into the Galo society at the grassroots level, it has definite influence on the decision-making process of the village *Keba* also. Thus, the respondents were asked, "Do you think that the party politics has influence on the *Keba* decision?" The response is given in the table 5.6.

The table (5.6) reveals that 50 per cent of the respondent leaders are of the view that party politics has significant influence on the village *Keba* in terms of decision-making. Only 20 per cent of the respondent leaders said that the party politics has no influence on the *Keba* decision. But 30 per cent of the leaders who said 'to some extent' also tacitly accept the influence of party politics on decision-making process of the village *Keba*, though such influence may be occasional and contextual. So, the responses of the leaders presented in the above table testify our assumption that party politics has influence on the *Keba* decision. The comparative analysis of the table reveals that relatively greater proportion of the modern leaders (53%) acknowledged the influence of the politics on the *Keba* decision when compared to the 47 per cent of the traditional leaders. The leader-wise break-up of the 'yes' percentage was 52 per cent among the Panchayat members, 63 per cent among the party leaders and 43 per cent among the church leaders, but in

Table 5.6. Distribution of the Respondents Showing Their Responses on Influence of Party Politics on *Keba* Decisions

Response	*Traditional leaders*				*Modern leaders*				
	GAM	*VE*	*PR*	*TL*	*PM*	*PL*	*CL*	*TL*	*G. TL*
Yes	32 (46)	15 (39)	8 (89)	55 (47)	24 (52)	19 (43)	12 (43)	55 (53)	110 (50)
No	16 (23)	8 (22)	1 (11)	25 (21)	9 (20)	2 (7)	8 (29)	19 (18)	44 (20)
To some extent	22 (31)	15 (39)	N	37 (32)	13 (28)	9 (30)	8 (29)	30 (29)	67 (30)
Total	70 (100)	38 (100)	9 (100)	117 (100)	46 (100)	30 (100)	28 (100)	104 (100)	221 (100)

case of the traditional leaders, it was 46 per cent among the *Gams*, 39 per cent among the village elders and 89 per cent among the priests. But, the 'No' percentage was proportionately higher (22%) among the traditional leaders when compared to the modern leaders (18%). The table further reveals that the difference in the proportion of the respondents who tacitly acknowledged the influence of politics on *Keba* decisions was very narrow. It was 32 per cent among the traditional leaders and 29 per cent among the modern leaders. Thus, the overall analysis of the table gives a clear indication of the influence of the party politics on decision-making process of the village *Keba* at present and the emerging leaders have better perception about the changing reality in the decision-making process.

PARTIALITY IN *KEBA* DECISION

For the purpose of our study, it is assumed that with the emergence of multiple centers of power in the village, the *Keba* decision is not always impartial. Taking this into account the respondents were asked, "Do you find any case of favoritism in the *Keba* decisions nowadays?" The response is given in the table 5.7.

As the table reveals, alarming proportion (65%) of leaders said that there is favoritism in the decisions of the *Keba*. Besides, 22 per cent of the leaders too believed that there are instances of favoritism in *Keba* decisions. The 'No' percentage is only 14 per cent. Thus, it is evident from this analysis that, unlike earlier, the *Keba* as an institution is under pressure, thereby erosion of the status as the only dispute resolution mechanism in the village. Such state of affairs is the by-product of the emergence of multiple centers of power in the village. The table further reveals that the 'Yes' percentage is relatively higher among the modern leaders (69%) when compared to the traditional leaders (61%). The respondents who said "to some extent" constituted 19 per cent of the modern leaders and 24 per cent of the traditional leaders. The 'No' percentage is higher (15%) among the traditional leaders than the modern leaders (12%). Thus, we may assume that the traditional leaders attached relatively greater degree of sanctity to the village *Keba* than

Table 5.7. Distribution of Respondents Showing Partiality in *Keba* Decision

	Traditional leaders				*Modern leaders*				
Responses	*GAM*	*VE*	*PR*	*TL*	*PM*	*PL*	*CL*	*TL*	*G.TL*
Yes	35 (50)	29 (76)	7 (78)	71 (61)	30 (65)	22 (73)	20 (71)	72 (69)	143 (65)
No	13 (19)	4 (11)	1 (11)	18 (15)	7 (15)	1 (3)	4 (14)	12 (12)	30 (14)
To some extent	22 (31)	5 (13)	1 (11)	28 (24)	9 (20)	7 (23)	4 (14)	20 (19)	48 (22)
Total	70 (100)	38 (100)	9 (100)	117 (100)	46 (100)	30 (99)	28 (99)	104 (100)	221 (100)

the modern leaders. However, the difference is marginally too narrow to provide any meaningful conclusion.

INFLUENCE OF WEALTH

It was assumed in our study that in the present context, the decision of the *Keba* is not always based on the merit of the cases. Apart from the influence of party politics, the wealthy people can also mould the *Keba* decision to some extent. It is forgone conclusion that wealth and power goes together. The common man in the village usually do not want to invite the displeasure of the rich man on minor pretext because, very often, the common people had to seek the help of rich man in times of crisis and disease. Hence, despite reservation, the common men may accommodate the decisions of the rich men while resolving various issues in the village. That is why, though the rich men cannot dictate the *Keba* decision in any way, but he may indirectly influence the decision by exerting pressure over the main decision-makers in the village. So, to know their opinion, the respondents were asked, "Do you think that the rich people can influence the *Keba* decision to their favour?" The response is given in the table 5.8.

The analysis of the table (5.8) reveals that the significant percentage (32%) of the total respondent leaders held the view that rich people can influence the *Keba* decision in their favour. Only 29 per cent of the total respondents said that the rich people cannot influence the decision of the village *Keba*. Further, 39 per cent of the respondents too tacitly accept the capability of the rich men to influence the *Keba* decision in the village. Hence, our earlier assumption that rich men can influence or mould the *Keba* decision is being testified to a great extent. The comparative analysis of the same table reveals that the percentage of leaders who said 'can influence' was comparatively higher among the modern leaders (34%) than the traditional leaders (31%). The leader-wise percentage was 30 per cent among the Panchayat members, 27 per cent among the party leaders and 46.43 per cent among the church leaders, whereas, in case of the traditional leaders, it is 34 per cent among the *Gams*, 26 per cent among the village elders and 22 per cent

Table 5.8. Distribution of the Respondents Showing Influence of Richman on *Keba* Decision

Response	*Traditional leaders*				*Modern leaders*				
	GAM	*VE*	*PR*	*TL*	*PM*	*PL*	*CL*	*TL*	*G. TL*
Can influence	24 (34)	10 (26)	2 (22)	36 (31)	14 (30)	8 (27)	13 (46)	35 (34)	71 (32)
Cannot influence	22 (31)	14 (37)	2 (22)	38 (32)	9 (20)	10 (33)	6 (21)	25 (24)	63 (29)
Considerably influence	24 (34)	14 (37)	5 (56)	43 (37)	23 (50)	12 (40)	9 (32)	44 (42)	87 (39)
Total	70 (100)	38 (100)	9 (100)	117 (100)	46 (100)	30 (100)	28 (100)	104 (100)	221 (100)

among the priests. But, in case of the leaders who said, "cannot influence" is proportionately higher (32%) among the traditional leaders when compared to the modern leaders (24%). The leader-wise break-up of this category was 31 per cent among the *Gams*, 37 per cent among the village elders and 22 per cent among the priests, but, in case of the modern leaders, it is 20 per cent among the Panchayat members, 33 per cent among the party leaders and 21.42 per cent among the church leaders. The proportion of the leaders who said, "considerably influence" or who tacitly acknowledges the influence of wealth on *Keba* decision is slightly higher among the traditional leaders (37%) in comparison to the modern leaders (32%). The leader-wise percentage was 34 per cent among the *Gams*, 37 per cent among the village elders and 56 per cent among the priest but in case of modern leaders, it was 50 per cent among the Panchayat members, 40 per cent among the party leaders and 32.15 per cent among the church leaders. Thus, it is observed through this analysis that though the proportion of difference in response was very thin, the emerging leaders could better perceive the changing trend in the decision-making process in the village *Keba*. The analysis of the above table further indicates that the sanctity and status of the village *Keba* as corporate and authoritative decision-making forum is under intense pressure. Unlike earlier, the *Keba* decision is not always transparent and conducive to the social harmony and justice. There is every possibility of justice being doctored, delayed or denied due to the influence of the wealth and the money power.

DISPUTE RESOLUTION

Generally, the village *Keba* used to be the only forum to settle any dispute. But it is observed that sometimes the aggrieved party take the case to the higher level like *Banggo Keba* under the Political Interpreter (PI), popularly known as '*Katakis*', at circle level or the district level or the court of Deputy Commissioner in-spite of the case being tried and decided in the village *Keba*. Taking this into account, the respondents were asked, "Where do you prefer to settle your dispute?" The response is given in table 5.9.

Table 5.9. Distribution of Respondents Showing Their Preference of Forum to Settle Dispute

	Traditional leaders				*Modern leaders*				
Responses	*GAM*	*VE*	*PR*	*TL*	*PM*	*PL*	*CL*	*TL*	*G.TL*
Village Keba	7 (100)	37 (97)	8 (89)	115 (98)	43 (94)	27 (90)	25 (89)	95 (91)	210 (95)
Banggo Keba	N	N	N	N	N	2 (7)	2 (7)	4 (4)	4 (2)
P.I. office	N	N	N	N	1 (2)	1 (3)	1 (4)	3 (3)	3 (1)
D.C. court	N	1 (3)	1 (11)	2 (2)	2 (4)	N	N	2 (2)	4 (2)
Total	70 (100)	38 (100)	9 (100)	117 (100)	46 (100)	30 (100)	28 (100)	104 (100)	221 (100)

The study of the table 5.9 reveals that in spite of the loosing faith on the righteousness of the *Keba* decision, almost all the leaders (95%) preferred to settle their dispute within village. To them, village *Keba* was more reliable than other forums of dispute resolution, and perhaps, the leaders considered that they could have better influence over the village *Keba*. The disputes when taken to higher forum become complicated and expensive which they wanted to avoid. The leaders, who prefer to take their dispute to the forums other than village *Keba* was very low and hence, do not reflect any specific representative opinion of the leaders. Only 1 per cent of the total respondents preferred to settle their dispute in P.I. office and 2 per cent each at *Banggo Keba* and the D.C. court. The table further reveals that relatively greater proportion (98%) of the traditional leaders preferred to settle their disputes in village *Keba* when compared to the modern leaders (91%). No traditional leaders preferred *Banggo Keba* and the P.I. office but 2 per cent and 1 per cent of the modern leaders preferred *Banggo Keba* and P.I. office respectively. In this analysis also, we can assume that relatively greater proportion of traditional leaders still have faith on the village *Keba* when compared to the modern leaders though the difference is marginal.

EDUCATIONAL BACKGROUND AND DECISION-MAKING

It has been reflected in many studies that the educational background is one of the most important determinants of the emerging leadership. In the context of changing rural scenario 'the effectiveness of the leaders largely depends on the level of education they possess'[11]. Since decision-making involves a rational choice of alternatives and integration of differing views into a workable agreement, it is assumed that the educated leaders are likely to be more conscious and rational to take right type of decision. In the traditional perspective, the decision-making processes regarding mainly the issues of judicial nature are based on customs, conventions, established norms and the collective conscience of what is wrong and what is right. But unlike

11. Mishra, S.N., *Politics and Leadership in Municipal Government*, Inter-India Publication, Delhi, 1979, p. 64.

earlier, the decision-making in the *Keba*, in the changing environment, is not always based on customs and conventions. In the present context, we cannot ignore the implicit or explicit influence of other factors like modern conception of justice based on codified law, official rules and regulations, popular judicial understanding and perception etc. over the decision-making process of the village *Keba*. Hence, in such circumstances, the educated people are likely to take better kind of decisions, because they are better exposed to the changing trends. Thus, to know their perception, our question was, "Do you think that educated people are more capable of taking decision in the village *Keba*?" The responses are given table 5.10.

According to the table (5.10), majority (53%) of the total respondents said that the educated persons are better equipped to take right kind of decisions in the society. The respondent leaders who said that the educated are 'less capable' constituted only 9 per cent of the total respondents. Their contention was that the educated leaders are not necessarily well conversant with the intricacies of tribal customary laws, which is the guiding factor in the *Keba* decision. However, 38 per cent of the leaders are of the opinion that education has nothing to do with decision-making and hence, they said that the educated and uneducated are equally capable in terms of decision-making skills. The leader-wise break-up of the table reveals that the leaders who said 'more capable' is proportionately higher among the traditional leaders (56%) in comparison to the modern leaders (50%). The leader-wise break-up was 51 per cent among the *Gams*, 58 per cent among the village elders and 78 per cent among the priests, but in case of modern leaders, it is 41 per cent among the Panchayat members, 50 per cent among the party leaders and 64 per cent among the church leaders. This particular analysis reveals that the traditional leaders, who are comparatively less educated, have greater degree of admiration for the educated people in the decision-making process, because now-a-days, the decisions are, in certain occasions, influenced by the modern judicial system and the official norms. The proportion of the leaders who said 'equally capable' is, on

Table 5.10. Distribution of the Respondents Showing Their Opinion on Educational Background and Decision-Making

	Traditional leaders				*Modern leaders*				
Response	*GAM*	*VE*	*PR*	*TL*	*PM*	*PL*	*CL*	*TL*	*G. TL*
More capable	36 (51)	22 (58)	7 (78)	65 (56)	19 (41)	15 (50)	18 (64)	52 (50)	117 (53)
Less capable	7 (10)	4 (11)	N	11 (99)	5 (11)	2 (7)	2 (7)	9 (9)	20 (9)
Equally capable	27 (39)	12 (32)	2 (22)	41 (35)	22 (48)	13 (43)	8 (29)	43 (41)	84 (38)
Total	70 (100)	38 (100)	9 (100)	117 (100)	46 (100)	30 (100)	28 (100)	104 (100)	221 (100)

the contrary, higher among the modern leaders (41%) when compared to the traditional leaders (35%). The leader-wise break-up of the respondents in this column was 48 per cent among the Panchayat member, 43 per cent among the party leaders and 29 per cent among the church leaders, but in case of the traditional leaders, it was 39 per cent among the *Gams*, 32 per cent among the village elders and 22 per cent among the priests. The percentage of leaders who said that the educated are less capable is proportionately equal (9%) each among the modern leaders and the traditional leaders. Amongst the traditional leaders, 10 per cent of the *Gams* and 11 per cent of the village elders said 'less capable' and no priest said that educated are less capable and the similar respondents among the modern leaders were 11 per cent among the Panchayat leaders, 7 per cent each among the party leaders and the church leaders. The overall analysis of the table reveals that the decision-making process is no more guided by the customs and tradition alone but, on many occasions, the decisions are influenced by other factors like modern concept of justice, official norms, party commands, etc. Hence, the educated leaders are likely to play more effective role in the decision-making process in the transitional Galo society.

DECISION-MAKING IN *KEBA* AND PANCHAYATS

The *Keba* is a traditional decision-making forum and decision is a product of lengthy deliberation and discussion without adopting a particular method of decision-making but the Panchayat is a formal and statutory institution in which decisions are taken by following certain procedural code. While the *Keba* is an informal and customary institution, the Panchayat is a formal and modern institution. There is no regular membership in *Keba*, any formal place and fixed time of meeting of the *Keba*. Every adult is the natural member of the *Keba* and it meets when need arises at any place preferably at the community hall (*Dere*) of the village. But in Panchayat, the members are formally elected and it meets, in principle, at regular interval at different levels. In the Panchayat meeting, the technical expertise and governmental guidance are always associated

Table 5.11. Distribution of the Respondents Showing the Difference in Decision-Making Between *Keba* and Panchayat

Response	*Traditional leaders*				*Modern leaders*				
	GAM	*VE*	*PR*	*TL*	*PM*	*PL*	*CL*	*TL*	*G.TL*
Yes	43	26	5	74	29	21	13	63	137
	(61)	(68)	(56)	(63)	(63)	(70)	(61)	(61)	(62)
No	27	12	4	43	17	9	15	41	84
	(39)	(32)	(44)	(37)	(37)	(30)	(54)	(39)	(38)
Total	70	38	9	117	46	30	28	104	221
	(100)	(100)	(100)	(100)	(100)	(100)	(100)	(100)	(100)

but the traditional *Keba* meeting is free from such official technicalities and state control and supervision. Taking these and other factors as background, we assumed that there is a certain degree of difference in the methods and means of decision-making in between the traditional village *Keba* and statutory modern Panchayat. Hence, the respondents were asked, "Is there any difference in decision-making between the *Keba* and Panchayat meeting?" The responses are given in table 5.11.

According to the table 5.11, the 62 per cent of the total respondent leaders opined that there is difference between traditional *Keba* and the modern Panchayat in terms of decision-making process. But, the substantial proportion (38%) of the leaders said that there is no difference. It is well understood that the Panchayats are considered as the grassroots level agency to take up developmental activities all over the country. However, it is not the same in case of Arunachal Pradesh. The developmental activities are usually taken up by the Anchal Samities. Since, in Arunachal Pradesh, the Gram Panchayats are practically not given any specific developmental functions, they rarely meet formally at this level[12]. Hence, the substantial numbers of respondents do not have the idea of Panchayat having separate meeting. The comparative study of the response represented in the above table reveals that the proportionate difference in the pattern of response between the traditional and modern leaders are very narrow though the 'yes' percentage is slightly higher among the traditional leaders (63%) when compared to the modern leaders (61%). The leader-wise break-up of the 'yes' percentage was 61 per cent among the *Gams*, 68 per cent among the village elders and 56 per cent among the priests, but in case of the modern leaders, it was 63 per cent among the Panchayat members, 70 per cent among the party leaders and 46 per cent among the church leaders. To know further about the difference in methods of decision-making between *Keba* and the Panchayat the leaders who said 'yes' were asked to indicate the difference.

---

12. See *Political Transition in the Grassroots in Tribal India* by A.C. Talukdar, Omsons Publication, Guwahati and Delhi, 1987, pp. 162-163.

Table 5.12. Distribution of Respondents Showing the Difference in Methods of Decision-Making Between *Keba* and the Panchayat

Methods	*Consensus*	*Majority*	*Arbitrarily by Leaders*	*Total*
Panchayat	30 (22)	73 (53)	34 (25)	137 (100)
Keba	75(55)	50 (36)	12 (9)	137 (100)

Note : This table reflects the opinion of 137 leaders who said that there is difference in decision-making between the *Keba* and Panchayat.

The table reveals an interesting phenomenon in the decision-making process of the Panchayat in relation to the village *Keba*. Only 22 per cent of the respondent leaders are of the opinion that the decisions are taken through consensus method in the Panchayat, whereas the majority (53%) of the leaders said that the decisions in Panchayat are taken by majority. Further, the substantial proportion (25%) of the respondent are of the opinion that decisions in the Panchayat are taken arbitrarily by the leaders. But in case of the *Keba* decisions, 55 per cent of the respondent leaders said that the decisions are taken in consensus, but 36 per cent of the leaders are of the opinion that the decisions are taken by majority in *Keba* also. Only 9 per cent of the respondents said that in *Keba* also, the decisions are taken arbitrarily by the leaders. The comparative study of the table (4.12) reveals that most of the decisions in the *Keba* is taken by consensus method but, in Panchayat, most of the decisions are taken on the majority principle. Further, the instances of arbitrary decision are higher in the Panchayat decisions when compared to the decision-making process of the *Keba*. Thus, we can assume that there is perceptible difference in methods of decision-making in between the traditional *Keba* and the modern Panchayat bodies. The decision-making process is more democratic in traditional *Keba* in comparison to the Panchayat meeting. There is greater participation of the people in the decision-making process of the village *Keba*. The decision being the product of lengthy deliberation, there is greater scope for consensus in *Keba* but the chances of majority or the arbitrary decision are comparatively lesser. But, in Panchayat, the final decisional product is, more often, influenced by party interest and the governmental supervision because, they are comparatively more exposed to the party politics and state bureaucracy. That's why, the instances of arbitrary decision is higher in the Panchayat decisions because, it is observed in many cases that the developmental priorities of a Panchayat area is determined by the higher level party leader like M.L.A. and the Panchayat leaders like Zila Parishad Member (ZPM). Under such circumstances, there are greater chances of arbitrary and discretionary decisions.

A decision, to be effective and reliable, must be acceptable not only to those who are party to the decision but also to the general population on whom the decision is likely to have an impact directly or indirectly. A decision becomes difficult to execute if the affected people do not accept it as appropriate. Thus, considering such perspective of decision, the workable decision would be the consensus decision because there is total unanimity on the decision and the execution of the decision would likely to be easy and spontaneous. However, it is not always easy and feasible to arrive at a consensus decision especially in a democratic polity where the right to dissent is always recognized. Hence, the best possible alternative is the majority decision, which is now considered as a universal trend in the modern democracies. The majority decision is one of the most practicable methods because there is scope of adjustment of the viewpoints of the minority too to represent their interest, so that a decision becomes acceptable to the wider sections of the society. The Galo village council (*Keba*) being democratic in its operational principles, the similar kinds of decision methods are in vogue. But, though democracy stands for the rule of majority, we cannot totally ignore the authoritarian elements in the decision-making process especially in the changing rural perspective. The emerging scenario in rural society is marked by a gradual emergence of educated elite and neo-rich class of people, who are becoming influential and instrumental in the decision-making process in the *Keba*. Such people usually enjoy good

Table 5.13. Distribution of the Respondents Showing Their Preference of Methods of Decision-Making

	Traditional leaders				*Modern leaders*				
Response	*GAM*	*VE*	*PR*	*TL*	*PM*	*PL*	*CL*	*TL*	*G. TL*
Majority	31 (44)	21 (55)	5 (56)	57 (49)	25 (57)	11 (37)	16 (57)	52 (51)	109 (50)
Consensus	38 (54)	15 (40)	4 (44)	57 (49)	16 (36)	13 (43)	9 (32)	38 (37)	95 (43)
Arbitrary by Leaders	1 (1)	2 (5)	N	3 (3)	3 (7)	6 (20)	3 (11)	12 (12)	15 (7)
Total	70 (100)	38 (100)	9 (100)	117 (100)	44 (100)	30 (100)	28 (100)	102 (100)	219 (100)

Note : Two Panchayat leaders did not respond the question.

rapport with the high officials and the higher-level party leaders. So, to serve their own interests, these new influential people may take arbitrary and authoritarian kind of decisions at certain juncture pertaining to certain issues in the village. So, to know the leaders' perception on this aspect, they were asked, "Which method of decision-making, according to you, is more reliable and effective?" The responses are given in table 5.13.

The analysis of the table 5.13 reveals that 50 per cent of the total respondent leaders preferred the decision by majority as most effective and reliable. These respondents are somehow, aware of the difficulty in arriving at a consensus decision in the changing context of the society. The respondents who preferred consensus decisions as more reliable and effective were 43 per cent of the total. Only 7 per cent of the respondents said that the arbitrary decisions taken by the leaders are practically more effective. Since consensus and majority decisions are difficult to arrive at, due to the rising expectations of the people and the multiplicity of interests among the different sections of the people, the arbitrary methods, sometimes, serve the purpose. The overall response in the above table reveals that the great majority of the leaders considered the democratic method of decision making like consensus and majority methods as more reliable and effective.

The comparative study of the response shows that the percentage of leaders who consider majority method as more effective was proportionately higher among the modern leaders (51%) when compared to the traditional leaders (49%), but the difference in proportion is very narrow. The leader-wise breakup on this variable was 57 per cent among the Panchayat member, 37 per cent among the party leader and 57 per cent among the church leaders but in case of the traditional leaders, it was 44 per cent among the *Gams*, 55 per cent among the village elders and 56 per cent among the priests. The percentage of leaders who considered consensus method as more effective is higher among the traditional leaders (49%) when compared to the 37 per cent of the modern leaders. The leader-wise breakup of the respondents on this variable was 54 per cent among the *Gam*, 40 per cent among the village elders and 44 per cent among the priests, but in case of modern leaders, it was 35 per cent among the Panchayat members, 43 per cent among the party leaders and 32 per cent among the church leaders. Hence, we can conclusively say that comparatively greater proportion of the traditional leaders consider the democratic method of decision-making as more effective and reliable in comparison to the modern leaders. Further, the percentage of the respondent leaders who considered arbitrary decision by the leaders as more reliable and effective is proportionately higher among the modern leaders (12%) when compared to the 3 per cent of the traditional leaders. The leader-wise breakup of the respondents who preferred arbitrary decision was 7 per cent among the Panchayat members, 20 per cent among the party leaders and 11 per cent among the church leaders but in case of the traditional leaders, it was 1 per cent among the *Gams*, 5 per cent among the village elders and no priest considered arbitrary decisions as reliable. One important trend in the response table is that the percentage of leaders who considered arbitrary decision as more reliable is highest among the party leaders (20%) but the leaders who considered the consensus method as more reliable is highest among the *Gams* (54%).

RELATIONSHIP BETWEEN *KEBA* AND PANCHAYAT

The loose system of Panchayat already exists in the traditional tribal society of Arunachal Pradesh. The people have a community spirit that runs through the entire social structure. Thus, introduction of the statutory Panchayat was simply aimed to formalize the existing system to give the people a sense of actual participation in the administration and development of the area so that the territory is integrated into the national mainstream, which was one of the guiding principle of the then NEFA administration. Since then, the traditional *Keba* and the statutory Panchayat is functioning side by side, sometimes, with overlapping role. But as an institution, there is conceptual difference between the two. The resolution of dispute or adjudication of justice

Table 5.14. Distribution of the Leaders Showing the Influence of *Keba* on Panchayat in Decision-Making

	Traditional leaders				*Modern leaders*				
Response	*GAM*	*VE*	*PR*	*TL*	*PM*	*PL*	*CL*	*TL*	*G. TL*
Yes	38 (54)	19 (50)	5 (56)	62 (53)	26 (57)	14 (47)	15 (54)	55 (53)	117 (53)
No	4 (6)	2 (5)	1 (11)	7 (6)	3 (7)	6 (20)	3 (10)	12 (12)	19 (9)
To some extent	28 (40)	17 (45)	3 (33)	48 (41)	17 (40)	10 (30)	10 (36)	37 (36)	85 (38)
Total	70 (100)	38 (100)	9 (100)	117 (100)	46 (100)	30 (100)	28 (100)	104 (100)	221 (100)

is totally out of the purview of the Panchayat bodies, whereas, it has been the responsibility of the *Keba* since times immemorial and it continues to take such decisions. The developmental issues, on the other hand, is taken by the Panchayat bodies at different levels though the leaders who are involved in such decision may equally play instrumental role in the judicial decisions of the *Keba* also. To seek their opinion, our question to the respondents was, "Can village *Keba* also influence the Panchayat bodies in the decision-making? " The responses are given in table 5.14.

The analysis of the table 5.14 reveals that the leaders who accept the influence of the traditional *Keba* on the Panchayat decisions constituted 53 per cent of the total respondents. These leaders are aware of the fact that though there is a role differentiation between the two, at the same time, they are influenced by each other in the decision-making process. Only 9 per cent of the respondent leaders said that the *Keba* cannot influence the Panchayat in the decision-making. But, the considerable percentage (38%) of the leaders said that the traditional *Keba* can influence the Panchayats in decision-making to some extent only. Those leaders also tacitly accept the influence of *Keba* over the Panchayat in decision-making process. The overall response of the leaders reveals that the traditional *Keba* influences the decisions of the Panchayat because, according to the table, only 9 per cent of the leaders said 'No' to the question. The comparative study of the table does not reveal any significant shift in the pattern of response between the traditional and modern leaders because the 'Yes' percentage was 53 per cent each among both the categories of leaders. But the 'No' percentage was proportionately higher among the modern leaders (12%) when compared to the traditional leaders (6%). The leader-wise breakup of the 'No' percentage was 7 per cent among the Panchayat members, 20 per cent among the party leaders and 11 per cent among the church leaders, but in case of the traditional leaders, it was 6 per cent among the *Gams*, 5 per cent among the village elders and 10 per cent among the priests. The leaders who said "to some extent" or those who tacitly accepted that the traditional *Keba* can influence the Panchayat decision is higher among the traditional leaders (41%) when compared to the modern leaders (36%). The leader-wise breakup of the respondents on this variable was 40 per cent among the *Gams*, 45 per cent among the village elders and 33 per cent among the priests, but in case of the modern leaders, it was 37 per cent among the Panchayat members, 33 per cent among the party leaders and 36 per cent among the church leaders. The analysis of the leader-wise pattern of response does not give a conclusive trend for meaningful generalization. But, the overall picture suggests that the traditional *Keba* can also influence the Panchayat bodies in the decision-making process.

SUMMARY

Our study on the opinion of the leaders regarding the decision-making process reveals a significant shift in the decisional methods and the ways and means to execute the decisions also. The usual traditional method of decision by consensus is being found to be gradually replaced by the majority methods and sometimes, with arbitrary and authoritarian method. The comparative analysis revealed that ironically, majority of the modern leaders at times tilted in favour of authoritarian and arbitrary decisions in the village. Further, *Keba*, the traditional decision-making forum, is coming under the intense pressure from the influence of money power and the politics and hence, *Keba* decisions are sometimes challenged. With the gradual erosion of the traditional authority, the young and educated people are becoming more and more instrumental in taking a decision in the village. However, though the instances of favoritism and partiality in the *Keba* decision is having a rising trend, the respondent leaders still prefer village *Keba* to other higher forum to settle the dispute. The study further shows that in terms of decision-making, there is certain difference between the *Keba* and the Panchayat. The *Keba* preferably take consensus decisions, but in the Panchayat, the decisions are taken through majority following certain procedures established by law. As the Panchayats are the institutional arrangement for democratic governance, gradually it is becoming more acceptable among the rural mass. The overall analysis shows that the legitimacy of the institution of *Keba* as the arbiter of dispute is gradually loosing its hold over the society and the emerging environment has facilitated the intrusion of the maladies of influence, favouritism and nepotism in the decision-making process.

6

Primordial Loyalties and Leadership

The numerous studies conducted on the rural and tribal leadership in India undisputedly subscribes to a common proposition that the emergence of leadership in rural and tribal society is basically based on ascriptive factors such as dominant caste, family background, hereditary status, age etc. But, at the same time, the scholars are equally unanimous on one aspect of leadership, that is, the emergence of new and younger leaders based on achievements and merits. Caste, on the basis of which the society is being organized in an institutional structural system, has been the chief source of power and authority in the Indian villages. Apart from the caste, other factors like family background, occupation, economic status etc. were the important factors in the emergence of leadership in the rural areas and some of them are still relevant in the rural context. The other indices of leadership, if closely examined, stem from the caste hierarchy. The dominant caste has still a privileged position in the Indian village in terms of an access to power and authority and other avenues of earning and learning though with reduced significance. However, due to the influence of the various agents of modernization, rapid change is perceivable in several arena of the rural life. In the rapidly changing rural scenario, new leaders are emerging who are drawn from larger sections of the society and whose bases are personal achievements rather than ascriptive factors. The pattern of rural leadership, as it exists today, reflects a transition from individual to collective, from hereditary to achievements and from ascriptive to functional type of leadership, the trend is to break away from the traditions and march towards rationality and efficiency, the hallmark of modernity. "The traditional village elders are either undertaking new functions and adjusting themselves with the emerging pattern or are being replaced after being rendered ineffective"[1]. But, the traditional determinants of leadership have not been totally jettisoned though the present trend is towards the new direction in the patterns of rural leadership and authority. "After all, the deep-rooted social traditions preserved through centuries in an agrarian society cannot be suddenly uprooted by state action or formally planned social policies. It is no wonder that in certain important level of rural leadership, some of its traditional determinants like the higher caste status are still powerful"[2]. But, the significance of traditional determinants of leadership like caste, family background, ritual status etc. are reduced to a great extent. "While the ascriptive principles still continue to be a potential force, they are increasingly being supplemented by achievement principles, and in the process, getting reduced to the position of being no more than contributory factors to status"[3]. In its traditional form, the caste system, as an ascriptive system of status and hierarchy, integrated society through ordering primary identities along a legitimized hierarchy of status, controlling all social, economic and political relationship in the society. The new political institutions, especially the adoption of adult franchise and the introduction of the Panchayati Raj institutions have brought in qualitative and quantitative changes in the traditional power structure. "The process of democratic decentralization virtually aimed at towards a shift from a highly centralized and elitist political system to a pluralistic and participant political system and thereby to bring the political opportunities nearer home to the masses

1. Rangnath, *Rural Leadership—Old and New*, 'in *Leadership in India*', Ed. L.P. Vidyarthi, Asia Publishing House, Bombay, 1968, p. 270.
2. *Ibid.* p. 275.
3. Mishra, S.N., *Political Socialization in Rural India*, Inter-India Publication, Delhi, 1980, p. 83.

and to make the leadership positions accessible to articulate political groups from different sections of society"[4].

The Galo society, in principle, does not recognize any hereditary elements in leadership formation though the traditional factors of power and influence always works as an impetus towards acquiring leadership in the village. There is no caste or rigid class division in the Galo society, hence, the concept of dominant caste or class is unknown. In such a classless society, the leadership does not rest with an individual person but with a collectivity of individuals in the village. Birth and descent may determine the status of a person, to some extent, but not the leadership formation. The decision-making on important issues is the responsibility of the *Keba*, which is a corporate body. Though practically, the deliberation in *Keba* is guided by some influential people and the elderly persons, every villager is, in principle, member of the *Keba* and everyone is party to the decisions taken. So, no single individual or separate body of individuals can assume the status of authority however gifted or influential he or they may be. Further, the Galos do not have the system of chief or headman in the village. It is wrong to conceive the *Gam* as village chief. Though functionally it is traditional, *Gam* has got an official status because he is appointed by the government. But the established official criteria for appointment of the *Gam* are not necessarily adhered to. It is generally conceived that a person of positive quality like having oratorical skill, balance of judgement, good knowledge of customary tribal laws and influential person is usually appointed as *Gam*, but it is almost impossible to officially determine such quality of a person. Hence, recruitment or appointment of the *Gam* may be motivated by primordial or other factors like recommendation from kin, lineage and clan groups, personal relationship with some officers of the district administration, recommendation from leader(s) of the political parties, economic status of a person, lobbying and pressure from other corners. This is true especially of the present trend of appointment of the *Gams* in Galo society.

4. Singh, R.S., *Rural Elites, Entrepreneurship and Social Change*, Rawat Publication, Jaipur, 1985, p. 81.

The appointment is being influenced by the said factor. The other village elders popularly known as *'Keba Abo'* or *'Nyikok'* acquire the status of a leader spontaneously over a long period of time. The oratorical skills, community zeal, knowledge of customary laws, balance of judgement etc. are the basic qualifying norms. The village elders have influence in the decision-making process due to their personal skills and achievements, and such qualities cannot be inherited. But many of the village elders are now appointed as *Gam*. The priest is a sacred leader and his role is separate and distinct. But, he can also take a leading role in other secular activities provided he has the requisite qualities to do so. The new entrants in the leadership category like panchayat leaders and the party office bearer are, in principle, democratically elected or selected leaders. They represent the modern democratic institutions. But, in case of the church leaders, some has got ascriptive status and others are achieved, because some of the Christian leaders are born Christian and some are converted. It is usually assumed that since Galo society is essentially democratic, the hereditary and other primordial factors have nothing to do with the emergence of leadership. Such assumption is further strengthened by the emergence of new leaders supposedly based on achievement and merit principles. But in our study, it is assumed that though Galo society is essentially democratic and the modern democratic norm has entered into the political process, the primordial and other factors, to a great extent, determine the recruitment of leaders, because generations have passed in a particular setting with a set cultural pattern and close attachment to the objects of nature such as the forest, rivulets, the spirits underlying the trees and shrubs, the animals and birds, the social taboos, do's and don'ts and so on. Hence, it would be misleading to ignore the influence of such factors on leadership formation. The lineage, clan and matrimonial relationships are also very strong in the Galo society, and such social environment, it is assumed, has an important bearing on the formation and emergence of leadership. The outstanding personal qualification with other supports from both intra-group and inter-group are an important ingredient of leadership. In spite of rapid socio-economic and political changes, the leadership process is not totally free from the influence of clan, kin group, family, neighbourhood etc. With this background in mind, the respondents were asked some questions.

FATHER'S STATUS

The study of the positions or status held by the leaders' father was considered necessary to understand the implicit hereditary principle in the status accorded to the leaders. It was assumed that the status of father is likely to have a definite impact on son's career. Though the hereditary principle in public office is never recognized in the Galo society, there are many instances that a son of a *Gam* becomes a *Gam* after the death of his father. Hence, the principle of succession in public office is maintained in many cases, consciously or unconsciously. Further, the Galos believe in the popular terms like *'Jikli'* (son of a priest becomes a priest), *'Kokli'* (orator's son becomes an orator), *'Abli'* (hunter's son becomes a hunter) etc. and it is evidently observed that son inherits the father's qualities in many cases. Whether it is genetically inherited or not is outside the scope of our study but it is popularly accepted in the Galo society. Such popular perception may pave the way for acceptance of hereditary aspects, though implicitly, in the leadership formation too. However, the information regarding the mother's status was not sought because, the Galo being a patriarchal society, she hardly plays a leadership role in the village. The role of women being limited or restricted in the public domain, she hardly can influence the child in leadership formation. Thus, to know the leaders' fathers' status or position in the village, the respondents were asked, "What position did your father held/hold in the village?" Their responses are presented in table 6.1.

The study of the table reveals that fathers of 70 *i.e.* 31 per cent of the total respondent leaders did not held any position in the society. Hence, their fathers have no influence on the present status of these leaders. But the fathers of majority 151 *i.e.* 69 per cent of the leaders held some position both formal and informal. The table further

Table 6.1. Distribution of the Respondents Showing the Position Held by Their Father

Position status	*Traditional leaders*				*Modern leaders*				
	GAM	*VE*	*PR*	*TL*	*PM*	*PL*	*CL*	*TL*	*G.TL*
Gam	13 (25)	10 (44)	1 (14)	24 (30)	11 (32)	10 (53)	7 (41)	28 (40)	52 (34)
Panchayat Member	3 (6)	1 (4)	N	4 (5)	4 (12)	N	3 (18)	7 (10)	11 (7)
Politician	4 (8)	1 (4)	N	5 (6)	5 (15)	1 (5)	N	6 (9)	11 (7)
Priest	6 (12)	1 (4)	3 (43)	10 (12)	6 (18)	1 (5)	N	7 (10)	17 (11)
P.I.	1 (2)	N	N	1 (1)	1 (3)	1 (5)	N	2 (3)	3 (2)
*Nyikok-Kokte**	24 (47)	10 (44)	3 (43)	37 (46)	7 (21)	6 (32)	7 (41)	20 (29)	57 (38)
Total	51 (100)	23 (100)	7 (100)	81 (100)	34 (101)	19 (100)	17 (100)	70 (101)	151 (99)

Note : This table shows the responses of 151 leaders whose father held certain position or status.

reveals that 34 per cent of the leaders' fathers were *Gam*, 7 per cent were politician, 11 per cent were the priest, 2 per cent were political interpreter and 38 per cent of the leaders' fathers were *Nyikok-Kokte*. Hence, most of the leaders' fathers were either *Gam* (34%) or *Nyikok-Kokte* (38%) and the rest are negligible in terms of number. The comparative study of the response shows that the total numbers of the leader whose father held a position is relatively higher among the traditional leaders. Yet it does not reveal any significant difference. But the comparative analysis of the specific post or position held by the leaders' father shows some important trend. The percentage of the leaders whose father was a *Gam* is proportionately higher among the modern leaders (40%) when compared to the traditional leaders (30%). The leader-wise percentage of modern leaders whose father was a *Gam* constituted 32 per cent among the panchayat member 53% among the party leaders and 41 per cent among the church leaders, but in case of traditional leaders, it is 25 per cent among the *Gams*, 44 per cent among the village elders and 14 per cent among the priest. The leaders who said that their father was a panchayat member was also proportionately higher among the modern leaders (10%) when compared to the traditional leaders (5%). The leader-wise proportion of the respondents whose father was a panchayat member constituted 12 per cent among the panchayat member and 18 per cent among the church leaders. But, in case of the traditional leaders, it was 6 per cent among the *Gam*, 4 per cent among the village elders and no priests' father or party leaders' father was a panchayat member. The son of the politician is also comparatively higher among the modern leaders (9%) when compared to the traditional leaders (6%). The leader-wise percentage of the respondents whose father was a politician constituted 15 per cent among the panchayat members and 5 per cent among the party leaders but in case of the traditional leaders, it is 8 per cent among the *Gams*, 4 per cent among the village elders and none of the priests and the church leaders were son of a politician. The son of the political interpreter is also comparatively higher among the modern leaders (3%) when compared to the traditional leaders (1%). Hence, proportionately the greater percentage of the modern leaders' father occupied the formal positions like *Gam*, panchayat member, party post and the political interpreter. But the son of the priest and the *Nyikok-Kokte* is proportionately higher among the traditional leaders when compared to the modern leaders. The proportion of the respondents whose father was a priest constituted 12 per cent among the traditional leaders and 10 per cent among the modern leaders. The leader-wise proportion of the son of the priest constituted 12 per cent of the *Gam*, 4 per cent of the village elders and 43 per cent of the priests but in case of modern leaders, it is 18 per cent of the panchayat members, 5 per cent of the party leaders and no church leaders were a son of a priest. In case of leaders who said that their father was a *Nyikok-Kokte* constituted 46 per cent among the traditional leaders and 29 per cent among the modern leaders. The leader-wise break-up of this variable is 47 per cent among the *Gams*, 44 per cent among the village elders, and 43 per cent among the priests, whereas among the modern leaders, it is 21 per cent among the panchayat member, 32 per cent among the party leaders and 41 per cent among the church leaders. One interesting finding of the analysis is that 43 per cent of the priests' fathers were priest, the highest proportion among different types of leaders who inherit the father's position. The analysis reveals that the position held by the father has some bearing on the emergence of leadership.

SOURCE OF INCOME OF LEADERS' FATHER

It was thought difficult to determine the income range of leaders' fathers as many of their fathers have already died and no record of income was left behind. The study of the source of income of leaders' father was, therefore, considered necessary because it would also reflect their income level and the main occupations. Agriculture being the principal occupation and main source of income, those who had allied source of income such as government contract works and private business were likely to have economically better status. Here, private business includes earning from the trading licence, selling of cane and bamboo products, sell of timber etc. Poverty and low income of the parents may depress the chances of the son's elevation to the position of influence in the society. " A major factor which influence the life chances of an individual is the economic status of the family of birth. An individual born in an affluent family has a better opportunity structure—better health, better education, better employment prospects, better social esteem—than one born of destitute parents"[5]. The leadership qualities can be developed better in an atmosphere where the individual can develop his faculties to the maximum extent, and the presence or absence of economic opportunities will determine, to a great extent, whether or not a person can play a leadership role specially in the present context of competition and conflict in the society. Hence, to know the economic status and occupation of the leaders' father, our question put to them was, "What was the main source of income of your father?" Their responses are in table (6.2) is analyzed.

The analysis of the above table reveals that almost all the leaders' fathers (95%) were dependent on agriculture as source of income and it was their main occupation too. Only 9 per cent of the leaders' father earned through government contract works and 5 per cent through private business. This shows that though the leaders' father might have been rich or wealthy in the indigenous term of cattle, land and traditional properties *(Adam-Tadok),* they were basically poor in the modern sense of the term because most of them were subsistence agriculturists. Thus, the fathers' source of income and occupation or the economic status has very limited influence on the present status of the leaders. The leader-wise break-up of the response reveals that the leaders who said that their fathers' income source was agricultural was proportionately higher among the traditional leaders (98%) when compared to the modern leaders (91%). The leader-wise break-up of the respondents whose father's source of income was agriculture constituted 97 per cent among the *Gams*, 100 per cent each among the village elders and the priests, but in case of the modern

5. *Social Background of Political Leadership in India,* Uppal Publishing House, Delhi, 1983, p. 102.

Table 6.2. Distribution of the Respondents Showing Their Father's Income Source

Source	*Traditional leaders*				*Modern leaders*				
	GAM	*VE*	*PR*	*TL*	*PM*	*PL*	*CL*	*TL*	*G.TL*
Agriculture	68 (97)	38 (100)	9 (100)	115 (98)	43 (93)	27 (90)	25 (89)	95 (91)	210 (95)
Govt. contract	1 (1)	4 (11)	N	5 (4)	1 (2)	2 (7)	1 (4)	4 (4)	9 (4)
Pvt. business	3 (4)	4 (11)	N	7 (6)	2 (4)	1 (3)	2 (7)	5 (5)	12 (5)

Note : Total is not given as some respondents indicated more than one source of income.

leaders, it was 93 per cent among the panchayat member, 90 per cent among the party leaders and 89 per cent among the church leaders. The leaders' father whose income source was government contract constituted 4 per cent each among the traditional leaders and the modern leaders respectively. The leader-wise break-up of the respondents on this variable constituted 1 per cent of *Gam* and 11 per cent of the village elders, along with the agricultural income, but the leader-wise percentage of modern leaders whose father earned from the government contract constituted 2 per cent of the Panchayat Members, 7 per cent of the party leaders and 4 per cent of the church leaders. The table further reveals that the proportion of the respondents whose father earned through private business was almost similar *i.e.* 6 per cent among the traditional leaders and 5 per cent among the modern leaders. The leader-wise break-up of this variable reveals that 4 per cent of the *Gams*' father and 11 per cent of the village elders' father earned through the private business but the percentage of the modern leaders whose fathers' income was private business constituted of 4 per cent of the panchayat member, 3 per cent of the party leaders and 7 per cent of the church leaders. It seems that the economic status of the father has slightly greater significance for the modern leaders but the difference in the pattern of response between the traditional and modern leader is too narrow to arrive at a meaningful generalization.

BASES OF LEADERSHIP

To know the factors, which mainly contributed to the leaders in acquiring the present position, four accepted variables were taken—economic status, family background, party support and the personal achievement. The personal achievement alone is not a sufficient ground for a person to emerge as leader rather; it should be accompanied by other factors like higher economic status, good family background and other support bases. Many studies on the rural and tribal leadership has amply demonstrated that the leaders are basically drawn from higher economic status, and it has greater significance for the emerging political leadership in the Galo society. "Money plays a dominant role not only in raising one to high positions in the politics but also in maintaining him in the power hierarchy"[6] . A generous rich person is always at the advantageous position of influence, because the general people look to him in an emergency and crisis situation. An individual from rich and influential family is also likely to have an added advantage to become a leader in the society and a member of a big family is also likely to participate more in the community affairs because, he is better assured of support from large number of family members and there is more person to share his physical labours at home. The support from a political party is equally one of the most important factors for emergence of a leader in the modern context. The party support has great significance for the emerging leadership like panchayat members and the party leaders because panchayat elections are now fought on party lines. But in the absence of distinct class of nobility based on birth, descent or otherwise in the Galo society, a person with a good reputation of honesty and integrity and those having positive qualities usually emerge as leaders in the long process. Such leaders are likely to be mass-based and enduring. Thus, to understand the contribution of these four factors towards leadership formation, the respondents were asked, "What factors help you most in acquiring the present status or position in the society?" Their responses are displayed in table 6.3 and analyzed subsequently.

As the table reveals, only 4 per cent of the total respondent leaders said that their economic status helped them in acquiring the present status of a leader. The proportion of leaders who said that their family background contributed most in becoming a leader constituted 14 per cent of the total respondents. 21 per cent of the leaders said that they are in the position due to the support of the political party. But, the majority (67%) of the leaders said that they acquired the present status of a leader because of personal achievement and individual merit. The analysis reveals that the ascriptive factors do not have great significance for the emergence of leaders in the Galo society. The economic

6. *Ibid.*

Table 6.3. Distribution of the Respondents Showing Their Bases of Acquiring Present Position

Factors (base)	*Traditional leaders*				*Modern leaders*				
	GAM	*VE*	*PR*	*TL*	*PM*	*PL*	*CL*	*TL*	*G.TL*
Economic status	2 (3)	3 (8)	N	5 (4)	N	1 (3)	3 (11)	4 (4)	9 (4)
Family background	10 (14)	6 (16)	2 (22)	18 (15)	6 (18)	5 (17)	3 (11)	14 (13)	32 (14)
Party support	11 (16)	5 (13)	N	16 (14)	14 (30)	7 (23)	10 (36)	31 (30)	47 (21)
Personal achievement	53 (76)	29 (76)	9 (100)	91 (78)	28 (61)	17 (57)	12 (43)	57 (55)	148 (67)

Note : The total is not shown as some respondents indicated more than one factor.

factor was very negligible in the leadership formation but during the course of interview, it was observed that there was a tendency, among the leaders, to project themselves as poor. The family background alone is not a sufficient criterion for a person to emerge as leader if he does not establish himself in the eye of the people by his good deeds. As table shows, the personal achievement is an important factor for recruitment of a person in the leadership process but the personal achievement, to some extent, is also conditioned by other ascriptive and the economic factors. It was also observed during the course of interview that the leaders tended to prefer personal achievement as the main factor for their rise to power and authority. Further, the party support is potentially an important factor for emergence of leadership.

The comparative analysis of the pattern of response reveals that the 'economic status' as a factor for emergence of leadership, has similar significance for the modern leaders *i.e.* 4 per cent among the traditional leaders and the modern leaders respectively. The leader-wise break-up of the respondents on this variable was 3 per cent among the party leaders and 11 per cent among the church leaders and in case of the traditional leaders; it was 3 per cent among the *Gams* and 8 per cent among the village elders. However, this difference does not reflect any important trend for close analysis. The 'family background' has slightly greater importance for the emergence of traditional leaders (15%) when compared to the 13 per cent of the modern leaders. The leader-wise break-up of the respondents whose main base was the 'family background' constituted 14 per cent among the *Gams*, 16 per cent among the village elders and 22 per cent among the priests whereas, in case of the modern leaders, it is 13 per cent among the panchayat members, 17 per cent among the party leaders and 11 per cent among the church leaders. But, in this particular analysis also, the difference in the proportion of respondents among the different types of leaders is too narrow to give an immediate conclusion. The table further reveals that the party support has greater significance for the emerging leaders because the percentage of leaders who said that 'party support' helped them most in acquiring the present position is proportionately higher among the modern leaders (30%) when compared to the traditional leaders (14%). The leader-wise break-up of the respondents whose base was the 'party support' constituted 30 per cent among the panchayat members, 23 per cent among the party leaders and 36 per cent among the church leaders, but in case of the traditional leaders, it was 16 per cent among the *Gam*, 13 per cent among the village elders and in case of the priests, their status is based on personal charisma. The percentage of leaders who said that they acquired the present position out of 'personal achievement' is proportionately higher among the traditional leaders (78%) when compared to the modern leaders (55%). The leader-wise break-up of the respondents on this variable was 76 per cent each among the *Gams* and the village elders and 100 per cent among the priests, whereas in case of the modern leaders, it is 61 per cent among the panchayat members, 57 per cent among the party leaders and 43 per cent among the church leaders. Hence, the personal achievement has greater significance for the traditional leaders when compared to the modern leaders.

VOTING BEHAVIOUR IN PANCHAYAT ELECTION

This particular study seeks to analyze the voting behaviour of the respondent leaders in the panchayat elections. It also attempts to find out the various factors, which determines the leaders' decision in favour of a particular candidate. Prior to the panchayat elections of 2003 in Arunachal Pradesh, the political parties were not legally permitted to contest the panchayat elections, however, behind the scene, it was always keenly contested among the political parties or between the rival leaders of the same party. But, under the framework of the Arunachal Pradesh Panchayati Raj Act, 1997, the political parties were legally permitted to field their candidates in the fray in the panchayat elections of 2003. In our study, it is assumed that the voting behaviour of the leaders are not necessarily guided by the party factor alone, though the election was contested by the candidates of different political parties. Along with the party factor, the family and clan relationship, integrity of the candidate and economic factors also determine the leaders' favour to a candidate. The bond of family, lineage and clan relationship is very strong in the Galo society, that's why, the village politics is vulnerable to such influences. In a multi-clan village, the clan loyalty may determine the political behaviour of a person but in single-clan village, the family and lineage consideration may influence the leaders' behaviour. It is also commonly observed that some leaders are active in politics for personal economic gain. The honesty and integrity of a candidate is a strong force in the village politics because there is comparatively greater degree of transparency in the village affairs. Thus, to know the guiding factors of leaders' political decision in favour of a candidate in the panchayat election, the question put to them was, "During panchayat election, what factors determines your decision if favour of a candidate?" Their responses are presented in table 6.4 and analyzed subsequently.

The analysis of the table reveals that mostly party loyalty and the integrity of the candidate determines the leaders' decision in favour of a candidate in the panchayat elections. 41 per cent of the leaders 'decisions are guided by the 'party factor' and 52 per cent of the leaders decisions in panchayat elections are guided by 'integrity of the candidate'. The percentage of leaders whose behaviour is guided by 'family-clan loyalty' and 'economic factor' in their voting bahaviour in panchayat election constituted of 8 per cent and 6 per cent respectively of the total. The analysis reveals that the ascriptive factors like family and clan loyalties are not significant determinants of the leaders' political behaviour in the panchayat election. The leader-wise break-up of the response does not show a definite shift in the pattern of response between traditional and modern leaders. The comparisons of the responses reveals that the greater proportions of the traditional leaders (42%) are guided by 'party loyalties' when compared to the 39 per cent of modern leaders. The leader-wise proportion of the respondents whose decisions are guided by the party factor constituted 41 per cent among the *Gam*, 42 per cent among the village elders

Table 6.4. Distribution of the Respondents Showing the Factors Influencing Their Decision in the Panchayat Election

	Traditional leaders				*Modern leaders*				
Factors	*GAM*	*VE*	*PR*	*TL*	*PM*	*PL*	*CL*	*TL*	*G.TL*
Party factors	29	16	4	49	22	8	11	41	90
	(41)	(42)	(44)	(42)	(48)	(27)	(39)	(30)	(41)
Family-clan	5	2	1	8	5	2	2	9	17
factor	(7)	(5)	(11)	(7)	(11)	(7)	(7)	(9)	(8)
Integrity of	33	20	3	56	26	18	15	59	115
candidate	(47)	(53)	(33)	(48)	(57)	(60)	(54)	(57)	(52)
Economic	5	2	1	8	4	2	N	6	14
factor	(7)	(5)	(11)	(7)	(9)	(7)		(6)	(6)

Note : Total is not shown as the respondents indicated more than one factor.

and 44 per cent among the priests, but among the modern leaders, it was 48 per cent among the panchayat members, 27 per cent among the party leaders and 39 per cent among the church leaders. The 'party loyalty' is the highest among the panchayat member and ironically lowest among the party leaders. The significance of family-clan loyalties is equivalent between the modern leaders and the traditional leaders (7% each). But the leaders guided by 'integrity of the candidate' are slightly higher (57%) among the modern leaders when compared to the traditional leaders (48%). The leader-wise break-up of the respondents whose decision in panchayat election is guided by the 'integrity of the candidate' was panchayat member : 57 per cent, party leaders : 60 per cent and church leaders : 54 per cent, but in case of the traditional leaders, it is 47 per cent among the *Gams*, 53 per cent among the village elders and 33 per cent among the priests. This difference in response can be attributed to the assumptions that the traditional leaders have little expectation of honesty and integrity from the party-based new leaders. The percentage of leaders who said their decision is determined by the 'economic factor' is slightly higher among the traditional leaders (7%) when compared to the modern leaders (6%). The leader-wise percentage of the respondents whose decisions are guided by economic factors constituted 7 per cent among the *Gams*, 5 per cent among the village elders and 11 per cent among the priests, but in case of the modern leaders, it is 9 per cent among the panchayat members, 7 per cent among the party leaders and no church leader is influenced by economic factors in the panchayat election. But the difference in the proportion of respondents among different types of leaders is too narrow to show an important leader-wise shift.

VOTING BEHAVIOUR IN THE ASSEMBLY ELECTIONS

We have already noted in the above table that the family-clan loyalties and economic factor are not very significant factor to determine the leaders' behaviour in the panchayat election but things may be different in the assembly elections. Thus, this particular study seeks to demonstrate the difference, if any, in the factors influencing the decision

Table 6.5. Distribution of the Respondents Showing the Factors Influencing Their Decision in Assembly Election

Factors	*Traditional leaders*				*Modern leaders*				
	GAM	*VE*	*PR*	*TL*	*PM*	*PL*	*CL*	*TL*	*G.TL*
Party factors	26 (37)	11 (29)	4 (44)	41 (35)	16 (35)	11 (37)	11 (39)	38 (37)	79 (36)
Family-clan factor	4 (6)	3 (8)	1 (11)	8 (7)	5 (11)	2 (7)	1 (4)	8 (8)	16 (7)
Integrity of candidate	38 (54)	23 (61)	3 (33)	64 (55)	26 (57)	16 (53)	15 (54)	57 (55)	121 (55)
Economic factor	5 (7)	3 (8)	1 (11)	9 (8)	8 (17)	2 (7)	1 (4)	11 (11)	20 (9)

Note : Total is not shown as the respondents indicated more than one factor.

in the panchayat and assembly elections. It was assumed that the determining factors for leaders' support to a candidate in a panchayat election may not necessarily be a determining factor in the assembly elections. Though elections at both the levels are organized on the party line, there is certain difference in environment in which the election is conducted. At panchayat level, the candidate has closer inter-personal relationship with the voters, but at the assembly level, such relationship is remote and distant. That is why; there may be variations in the factors, which determine the cause for leaders' support to a candidate. With this background in mind, the respondent leaders were asked, "During Assembly election, what factor determines your decision in favour of a candidate?" The responses are given in table 6.5 and analyzed below.

As the table shows, 36 per cent of the respondent leaders said that they support a candidate in assembly election out of 'party loyalty'. 7 per cent of the leaders said that they support a candidate due to 'family or clan affinities'. The proportion of leaders who extend support due to the 'integrity of the candidate' constituted of 55 per cent of the total respondents and that of 'economic factor' is 9 per cent of the total. It reveals that family-clan loyalties and profit motive is not a significant factor to determine the leaders' support to a candidate in assembly election also, rather the leaders' support of candidate is based on 'party loyalties' and 'integrity of the candidate'. The leader-wise break-up of the response does not reveal any important shift for meaningful studies. The leaders who support an assembly candidate out of the 'party loyalty' constituted 35 per cent among the traditional leaders and 37 per cent among the modern leaders—the leader-wise break-up was 37 per cent among the *Gams*, 29 per cent among the village elders, 44 per cent among the priests and among the modern leaders, it was 35 per cent of the panchayat members, 37 per cent of the party leaders and 39 per cent of the church leaders. Those who are guided by 'family or clan affinities' were 7 per cent among the traditional leaders and 8 per cent among the modern leaders. The leader-wise proportion of respondents who extend support out of 'family-clan loyalties' among traditional leaders are—*Gam* : (6%), village elders : (8%), priests : (11%) and among the modern leaders are—panchayat members : (11%), party leaders : (7%) and the church leaders : (4%). As per the table, 8 per cent of the traditional leaders and 9 per cent of the modern leaders are guided by the 'economic factor' or personal gain. The leader-wise proportion of the respondents who are motivated by the economic prospects constitute, among traditional leaders—*Gams* : (7%,) village elders : (8%), priests : (11%) and that of the modern leaders—panchayat members : (17%), party leaders : (7%) and church leaders : (4%). But the leaders who admitted that they support a candidate in Assembly election due to the 'integrity of the candidate' constituted 55 per cent each among the traditional leaders and the modern leaders respectively. The leader-wise percentage of the respondents on this variable constituted 57 per cent among the panchayat members, 53 per cent among the party leaders, 54 per cent among the church leaders but in case of traditional leaders, it is 54 per cent among the *Gams*, 61 per cent among the village elders and 33 per cent among the priests. The leader-wise variation in the proportion of the respondents is too narrow to draw a conclusive observation. Further, the degree of significance of the determinants of support are almost similar in both panchayat and assembly elections. The respondent leaders gave similar type of response in a different situation of choosing a leader. Even then, the party factor has slightly greater relevance for panchayat election (41%) when compared to the assembly election (36%). Though little differences are there, it does not lead to any significant change. But, the overall analysis reveals that the family-clan loyalties and economic factor don't influence the leaders' political behaviour in a big way. The man of honesty and integrity is liked by the majority of the respondents.

POSITIONS HELD BY THE IN-LAWS

The matrimonial relationship is an important cohesive factor in the traditional Galo society. In earlier days, many instances of inter-clan feuds were compromised by the compulsions of matrimonial relationships. Since traditional marriage system of the Galos involves lot of 'give and take' between the two families, matrimonial relationship is an enduring affair. Such relationship is remembered, if not maintained, even after the lapse of the generations in the form of narration and hymns by the priest on the socio-religious occasions and thus, the emotional attachment continues between the descendants of the two families. As the Galos have usually the practice of negotiated marriage system, the groom's family always prefer a bride from wealthy family or one who has three-four brothers so that they (groom's family) are assured of help in the event of crisis or disease or further, assured of quality items *(Adam-Tadok)* in the process of 'give and take' associated with the marriage. There are lots of instances that the brides' family contributed much to the status of a person in the society. The son-in-law or brother-in-law of a rich and influential person get his social esteem elevated and get implicit or explicit social and economic protection. Thus, our assumption was that the position held by the leaders' in-laws also help them (respondents) in acquiring the present status. This study would also reveal the implicit or explicit contribution of the wives in acquiring the present status of the respondents. The following table 6.6 shows that position or status held by the leaders' father-in-law or brother-in-law.

The table reveals that the majority (56%) of the leaders' father-in-laws or the brother-in-laws (henceforth the 'in-laws') held certain position or status in the society. The in-laws who were an ordinary citizen constituted of 44 per cent only. Among the leaders' in-laws, who held a position or status, 21 per cent were *Gam*, 10 per cent were panchayat member, 7 per cent were politician and 18 per cent of the total were the rich man, thus, the maximum of them were *Gam*. It reveals that the leaders preferably choose wives or brides from the family of higher status and this might have contributed positively to the present status of the leaders. The leader-wise break-up of the response reveals that the percentage of leaders whose in-laws held a position was proportionately higher among the modern leaders. But the greater proportion (50%) of the traditional leaders' in-laws

Table 6.6. Distribution of the Respondents Showing the Position Held by Their In-Laws

Position/ status	*Traditional leaders*				*Modern leaders*				
	GAM	*VE*	*PR*	*TL*	*PM*	*PL*	*CL*	*TL*	*G.TL*
Gam	10 (14)	6 (16)	2 (22)	18 (15)	13 (28)	8 (27)	7 (25)	28 (27)	46 (21)
Panchayat Member	8 (11)	5 (13)	N	13 (11)	2 (4)	3 (10)	5 (18)	10 (10)	23 (10)
Politician	4 (6)	2 (5)	N	6 (5)	6 (13)	3 (10)	N	9 (9)	15 (7)
Richman	16 (23)	5 (13)	1 (11)	22 (19)	8 (18)	3 (10)	6 (21)	17 (16)	39 (18)
Commoner	32 (46)	20 (53)	6 (67)	58 (50)	17 (37)	13 (43)	10 (36)	40 (38)	98 (44)
Total	70 (100)	46 (100)	9 (100)	117 (100)	46 (100)	30 (100)	28 (100)	104 (100)	221 (100)

was the common man when compared to the in-laws of the modern leaders (38%). The comparative study of the positions held by the leaders' in-laws reveals that the greater proportion (27%) of the modern leaders' in-laws was *Gams* when compared to the traditional leaders (15%). The proportion of the respondent leaders whose in-laws were the panchayat member was but slightly higher (11%) among the traditional leaders than the modern leaders (10%). The politician among the leaders' in-laws was higher (9%) among the modern leaders than the traditional leaders (5%). Compared to the 19 per cent of the modern leaders, 16 per cent of the traditional leaders' in-laws were the rich men. The comparative analysis reveals that the leaders' in-laws who held a position or status in the villages were relatively higher among the modern leaders when compared to the traditional leaders. Thus, the overall analysis indicates that the modern leaders are likely to get more support from their in-laws in acquiring the present status in the society.

CONTRIBUTION OF THE IN-LAWS

As shown in the above table and its analysis, the majority of the leaders' in-laws occupied certain position or enjoyed certain status in the society. So, to prove the definite contribution of the in-laws in acquiring the present status or position of leaders, the respondents were asked, "Did the in-laws contribute you in any way in acquiring the present position?" Their responses are given in the table 6.7 and analyzed subsequently.

As the table reveals, the significant proportion (42%) of the total respondents confessed that the family members of their wife (henceforth in-laws) contributed in acquiring the present status. The 'No' percentage is only 39 per cent of the total. But, 19 per cent of the leaders who said "to some extent" implicitly accepted the contribution of the in-laws in acquiring their status. Hence, the table confirms our assumption regarding the positive contribution of the in-laws in acquiring the leadership status of the respondents. The comparative analysis of the responses reveals that the 'Yes' percentage is comparatively higher (46%) among the modern leaders when compared to the traditional leaders

Table 6.7. Distribution of the Respondents Showing the Contribution of In-Laws to Their Status

Response	*Traditional leaders*				*Modern leaders*				
	GAM	*VE*	*PR*	*TL*	*PM*	*PL*	*CL*	*TL*	*G.TL*
Yes	27	19	N	46	18	15	15	48	94
	(39)	(50)		(39)	(39)	(50)	(54)	(46)	(42)
No	34	10	9	53	16	8	9	33	86
	(49)	(26)	(100)	(45)	(35)	(27)	(32)	(32)	(39)
To some extent	9	9	N	18	12	7	4	23	41
	(12)	(24)		(16)	(26)	(23)	(14)	(22)	(19)
Total	70	38	9	117	46	30	28	104	221
	(100)	(100)	(100)	(100)	(100)	(100)	(100)	(100)	(100)

(39%). The leader-wise break-up of the 'Yes' percentage constituted 39 per cent among the panchayat members, 50 per cent among the party leaders and 54 per cent among the church leaders, but in case of traditional leaders, it is 39 per cent among the *Gams*, 50 per cent among the village elders and no priest said that their in-laws contributed to their present status. The 'No' percentage is conversely higher (45%) among the traditional leaders when compared to the modern leaders (32%). Those who tacitly accepted the contribution of the in-laws are proportionately higher (22%) among the modern leaders when compared to the traditional leaders (16%). The overall analysis of the table reveals that the leaders who got support from the in-laws is proportionately higher among the modern leaders and such difference can be attributed to the fact that a status of a person as priest in Galo society is purely a personal achievement and considered as 'God gifted'. As it is socially accepted, neither a person can be trained in priesthood nor can it be learnt.

TYPES OF CONTRIBUTION

It is assumed that the wealthy in-law can give monetary support to daughter's family at the time of crisis, election and important socio-religious occasions, thereby; help him in enhancing the self-esteem. The influential in-laws may provide income opportunities by which a person may get a chance to acquire better economic status. Since, matrimonial relationship is very strong in Galo society, the in-laws family virtually act as the lobbying-agent of the grooms on various occasions. The following table displays the types of contributions made by the leaders' in-laws.

The table reveals that 15 per cent of the leaders, out of 135 respondents, got monetary help from the in-laws' family and 16 per cent of the leaders were provided with source of earning or income opportunities by their in-laws. 26 per cent of the leaders got support from the in-laws in form of lobbying and other moral support and 43 per cent of the leaders got 'other' contribution in the form of customary presentation of ornaments and casual help in the event of

Table 6.8. Distribution of the Respondents Showing the Type of Contribution by the In-Laws

	Traditional leaders				*Modern leaders*				
Contribution	*GAM*	*VE*	*PR*	*TL*	*PM*	*PL*	*CL*	*TL*	*G.TL*
Financial help	7 (19)	5 (18)	N	12 (19)	4 (13)	2 (9)	2 (11)	8 (11)	20 (15)
Income opportunity	4 (11)	4 (14)	N	8 (12)	6 (20)	5 (23)	3 (16)	14 (20)	22 (16)
Lobbying	12 (33)	6 (21)	N	18 (28)	6 (20)	7 (32)	4 (21)	17 (24)	35 (26)
Other	13 (37)	13 (47)	N	26 (41)	14 (47)	8 (36)	10 (52)	32 (45)	58 (43)
Total	36 (100)	28 (100)	N	64 (100)	30 (100)	22 (100)	19 (100)	71 (100)	135 (100)

Note : This table represents the response of 135 leaders who accepted the contribution of their in-laws' family in acquiring the present status.

crisis which may not have necessarily contributed to the leaders in acquiring higher status but could have been necessary to maintain the normal matrimonial relationships. The comparative study of the responses in various columns suggests that the total percentage of the respondents who got support from the in-laws was relatively higher among the modern leaders when compared to the traditional leaders. Such difference in the proportion may be attributed to the fact that among the traditional leaders, the priests did not get any support from the in-laws because their status in the society is purely on the achieved principle. Whereas, the close analysis of the table reveals that those who got financial support from the in-laws were proportionately higher (19%) among traditional leaders than the modern leaders (11%). At the same time, those who were given 'income opportunities' by the in-laws was relatively higher (20%) among the modern leaders when compared to the traditional leaders (12%). The proportion of the respondents whose in-laws lobbied for them constituted 28 per cent among the traditional leaders and 24 per cent among the modern leaders and those who got other kinds of support constituted 41 per cent among the traditional leaders and 45 per cent among the modern leaders. As the overall picture of the table reveals, the status of the in-laws has a bearing on the leaders' status, which signifies that leaders' wives also, though not instrumentally, contributed to the leaders in acquiring their present positions or status in the society.

SUMMARY

The study of the leaders' response in this chapter reveals that the parental position has important bearing on the emergence of present leadership, because, majority of the leaders' father held some position or status in the village. The formal position of the father had relatively greater significance for the emerging leadership. The study further reveals that party support, personal achievement and the integrity, etc. are the most important bases of leadership out of the variables covered in this study. Besides, the in-laws' support is also a factor in the emergence of the leader because majority of the leaders' in-laws held some position or status and substantial proportion of the respondents confessed that they got support from the in-laws' family in acquiring or maintaining the present position. But, the overall analyses of the response show that the primordial factor has very limited role in the leadership formation and this can be attributed to the relative homogeneity of the Galo society.

7

Conclusion

Since the leaders are usually considered as precursor to change and development, the study of leadership is an important dimension to understand the emerging socio-political system and the nature of transition taking place in the society. This study is an attempt to understand the emerging trends of leadership in Arunachal Pradesh with special reference to Galo society. Arunachal Pradesh being a late entrant into the modern democratic and representative politics, the traditional political institutions of the respective tribes were the only forum for community decision-making and mechanism to regulate the society. The functioning of these tribal councils were guided by the traditionally influential village leaders like *Gaon Burah* (popularly known as *Gam*) and other village elders; and the decisions were based on the customary laws of the land. But with the introduction of statutory panchayats and the emergence of party politics, a new trend has emerged in the grassroot leadership pattern. Now, what we observe in the village is the emergence of multiple centres of power and decentralized decision-making authority; and in the process, the status of the *Gam* and other village elders appears to be significantly eroded.

The study of leadership has attracted the interest of the sociologists, political scientists and social psychologists alike because the growing complexities of life, advancement in science and technology, increasing role of the government, rising expectations of the people and other similar factors have exalted the social significance of the study of leadership. However, there is no unanimity among the writers on the concept of leadership. Basically, there are three popular theories of leadership. Firstly, the Trait Theory tends to view the leadership as a special trait or in-born qualities, which predestine him to be a leader. According to this concept, the leaders are born; not made. Secondly, the Situational Theory maintains that leadership is a relationship that exists between persons in a social situation. It does not reside in a person; rather, it is the function of whole situation. A person who is a leader in one situation may not necessarily be a leader in other situation. Thirdly, the Group Theory of leadership maintains that leadership is a functional relationship between three basic variables *viz.*, the leader, the group and the situation. However, each concept taken separately reveals only a part of the total phenomenon but they have their share of contribution to the study of leadership.

The present work is an attempt to study the emerging trend of leadership at the grassroots level under the impact of the forces of modernization. Besides that, the study also throws a light on the process of socio-political transition taking place at the village level in light of the rapid democratization of the rural society. The real value of such a study does not necessarily lie in the degree of validity of its conclusions for wider areas, rather, it is of particular value in that it spotlights the complexities of the emerging situation. Apart from the participant observation of an insider, this study is basically based on the responses of 221 respondent leaders selected from fifteen different Galo villages spreading over five administrative circles of both the East and West Siang districts.

As the study reveals, the socio-economic background of an individual has significant bearing on the emergence of leadership; but many of the traditionally important determinants of leadership are no more significant especially for the emerging pattern of leadership. Hence, there has been perceptible change in the leadership pattern in terms of its determinants, though certain traditional factors are still relevant. The leadership in Galo society is predominantly a male affair, however, the emerging leadership have relatively more women representative among them. The seniority in age is no more an important criterion of leadership as it used to be and the rural leaders are not necessarily drawn from the large family and it is true especially of the emerging leaders. However, the educational background of an individual, which was never a factor of leadership in the traditional Galo society, is one of the most important determinants of leadership in the emerging situation. The occupation and income too is not a significant factor for general leadership formation, because, almost all of the leaders are agriculturist by occupation. Besides, most of them are from low and moderate-income group in terms of rupees, which is a general characteristic of a rural economy. However, the comparative analysis shows that the modern leaders have slightly higher income and multiple sources of income, because, many of them are found to be engaged in allied occupation apart from the agriculture. The economic status is necessary not only for emergence of the leadership but also for the maintenance of leadership status. As indicated by the study of variables like movable property, landholding, mode of cultivation, type of dwelling house, *Togu* celebration and the generosity of the leaders etc., the leaders are usually drawn from the higher economic status. At the same time, there is significant difference between the modern and traditional leaders so far as the indicators of the economic status is concerned. For example, the modern leaders relatively own more modern assets and live in modern house in comparison to the traditional leaders. The assets of the modern leaders are mostly inherited rather than acquired by them. The study further reveals that the traditional leaders are wealthier in terms of the indigenous items like cattle, poultry, traditional properties (*Adam-Todok*) etc. and that is supported by the study of '*Togu*' performed by the leaders in their lifetime. Though the '*Togu*' celebration is an expensive affair, those who perform '*Togu*' twice or thrice is proportionately higher among the traditional leaders, which suggest that they are wealthier in the traditional perspective than the modern leaders. The leaders are found to be generous because, the majority of them have donated generously on many occasions in the village, which also suggest that they are economically sound to do so. It is rightly stated that shortsightedness or selfishness may make a person rich and influential but not a leader in any case. This is especially true of the party-based new leaders who are supposed to maintain their support base for future political career. Thus, generosity is an important aspect of the rural leadership. Our analysis on some aspect of political socialization of the leaders reveals that they are politically active and conscious. The leaders are active participants in the modern political process. Unlike earlier, their level of influence is no more confined to the respective village only and that is true especially in case of the modern leaders. Apart from being a member of one political party or the other, the leaders have membership in various clan-based or welfare-based or the religion-based associations or unions. However, the modern leaders are found to be more secular and broad-based in their institutional affiliation. Further, the leaders have satisfactory access to the radio, which is supposed to bring progressive orientation among them. However, they have limited exposure to the newspaper due to the low level of educational attainment and the lack of circulation. The modern leaders are likely to have better awareness and knowledge about the contemporary situations, because, they are relatively better informed and more adequately exposed to the mass-media. The close study of the socio-economic backgrounds of the leaders shows that the leadership of an ascriptive kind tends to disappear, and it gradually gravitates into the hands of groups, which are a little more advanced in occupation or slightly better placed in regard to economic power than the rest. The power and authority in the village tends to shift into the hands of those who are neo-rich or educated, or have 'connections' with the government officials or influential members of the ruling political parties.

The study further reveals that the attitudes and perceptions of the leaders are basically in tune with the changing socio-political environment except in respect of few issues where the traditional values still hold strong position. The attitude and perception of the leaders in regard to some important customary practices and other social issues like marriage, marriage celebration (*Togu*), status of women, social taboos, etc. reflects a progressive change towards modernization and rationality. The leaders are ready to accept the inter-tribal marriage and none of them prefer child marriage. This is certainly a great breakthrough in the traditional outlook and values of the rural community. A look at the leaders perception on *Nyame-Renam* and *Omeh Areh* (bride-price) indicates that most of them are in favour of giving up the derogatory social practices, and the emerging leaders are more progressive in outlook in this connection. However, the substantial proportion, generally, of the traditional leaders are in favour of the retention of these system and hence, are nostalgically backward looking. There are certain people who are not conversant with the modern ideas and persistently sticking to old ideas and institutions and stand for the old values. The majority of the leaders do not like the practice of slaughtering of mithun in the name of marriage celebration and existing social taboos. On the basis of our study, we are inclined to say that the emerging leaders are more progressive and broadminded in their outlook. On the question of the sex of the first child and daughters' right to inheritance, the leaders relatively maintain a rigid stand in favour of the male child, which is a clear reflection of the traditional patriarchal society. However, in matters of giving formal education to the children, the majority of the leaders do not discriminate between the male and female child. Further, our findings in regard to the leaders' perception on some gender-related issues like widow-remarriage, role of women in *Keba*, appointment of women as *Gam* and reservation for women in the panchayat bodies indicates that the women are never treated lowly in the tribal society. The majority of the leaders have positive opinion in favour of the widow-remarriage, though few of them did not give clear answer. Though the women practically do not take part in the *Keba* deliberation, most of the leaders are not averse to their taking part in the same. The capability of the women to participate in the process of arbitration is recognized by the majority of the leaders. Most of the leaders do not have biasness against the recruitment of women to the post of *Gaon Burah/ Gam*, which suggest that the women too can play a leading role in the decision-making process in the *Keba*. The leaders are equally liberal on the question of reservation of seats for women in the panchayat bodies. Majority of them are in favour of the reservation. Thus, our analysis indicates that many traditional moorings attached to the status of women are sinking in the waves of the present environment. The majority of the leaders are gender-neutral. However, few of them were found to be trapped between the traditional ethos and the modern sense of justice and equality. In almost all the variables, the emerging leaders are found to be more progressive and broad-minded than the traditional leaders. The study reveals the forging of a new synthesis between the old and the new without major emotional disturbance or turmoil in the inter-group behavioural pattern. Though the traditional belief system still holds importance inspite of the changing environment, there is a definite shift in the value-orientation and perceptions of the leaders. The social outlook of the leaders shows sign of an appreciation for modernization and change. The new ideas have gradually penetrated into their social structure, which slowly found root in their value perception. Further, the leaders' perception on the village leadership and the present state of the *Keba* reveals that the popularity and acceptance of the *Gam* as leader of the village has diminished to a great extent and consequently, the status of the traditional village council (*Keba*) as the mechanism of arbitration and decision-making, is gradually declining. Though the *Gams* remains to be relatively more popular and influential leader in the village affairs, but with reduced acceptance. The party-based new leaders are emerging as powerful and influential at the cost of the status of the *Gams*. Thus, our analysis shows the emergence of multiple centres of power at the grassroot level. However, there is tendency among the different types of leaders to assert their own status, which indirectly suggests that a sort of competition is going on between the traditional and the modern leaders. Among other factors, the introduction of the statutory panchayats in the rural villages have been instrumentally responsible for the erosion of power and prestige of the *Gams* and the majority of the *Gams* themselves openly or tacitly accepted this fact. The institution of village *Keba*, which was responsible for the regulation of village lives is changing its character. Moreover, where they were once guided by the *Gams* and elders, they have now become progressively subjected to democratic control at least in principle. But, in spite of the diminishing authority of the traditional leaders, the common people have still faith on *Keba*, may be due to the lack of alternative indigenous forum of conflict resolution. Our analysis further confirms that there has been major shift in the leadership pattern in terms of its determinants. The educational background is found to be the most important determinant of leadership followed by integrity-honesty, party supports and others. The family background and the knowledge about tradition is no more the guiding factor of emergence of leadership in the village, rather, leadership, at present or in future, tends to shift towards those who are educated and dynamic.

The analysis of the decision-making process in context of the changing pattern of leadership reveals a significant shift in the methods of decision-making process and the ways and means to execute the decisions. Though the leaders usually adopt the democratic method of decision-making, the traditional method of decision by consensus is being slowly replaced by the modern method of decision by the majority and at times, by the decisions arbitrarily taken by the leaders. Since the traditional customs are exposed to modern values and the old relationships are strained, the *Keba* decisions are not always guided by the traditional spirit of simplicity and truthfulness, rather, there are instances of arbitrary decisions. In the present context, the decision by consensus is not always practically feasible or possible. Further, due to the informal nature of the village *Keba* and the absence of separate organ for execution of its decisions, the leaders usually resort to persuasion method to execute the *Keba* decisions. The leaders usually adopt the democratic method of influence while discharging leadership role in the village *Keba*. However, the substantial proportion of them admitted that they adopt undemocratic means like political and family-clan pressure. One of the important finding of our analysis is that in terms of decision-making process, the traditional leaders are more democratic in approach than the modern leaders. This can be attributed to the fact that in developmental issues in which the role of the modern leaders are more prominent, their decisions are often guided by the party interest or the dictates of the so-called high command. Thus, the decisions sometimes become undemocratic and arbitrary because the diverse and conflicting interest of the political parties, influential people, official formalities, etc. are to be accommodated while taking a decision on developmental issues. On the other hand, the village *Keba* being a customary institution facilitates relatively greater scope for discussion and deliberation, which paves the way for more democratic decision-making. However, the majority of the leaders openly or tacitly conceded that there is a growing tendency among the common men to disobey the *Keba* decisions. The *Keba* decisions are sometimes challenged and appealed for adjudication at the higher forums, which indicates that there is a gradual decline in the influence and legitimacy of the village *Keba* and its leadership. In the process, the tribal mode of justice is no more quick, simple and free of cost as its used to be, because, the 'money' and 'power' also play a significant role in the process of adjudication of justice in the *Keba*. Besides this, the *Keba* decisions are not always free from the influence of the party politics. The role of the politician is very much extended. They are gradually elbowing out the leaders of the society; and a democratic polity can hardly avoid the influence of the ruling party politician representing the villages. Further, the rich and wealthy people can also exert significant influence over the decision-making process of the *Keba*. To a great extent, they can influence or mould the *Keba* decision. The power system in the village has a tendency to incline in favour of the individuals or groups who can control the economic expectations of the people. Thus, the emergence of multiple centres of power has facilitated the gradual intrusion of the maladies of influence, favouritism and nepotism in the indigenous decision-making mechanism. Moreover, the loyalty of the people, which was previously fixed in one corporate determinant body of persons, has now been split into 'loyalties' to a number of bodies and persons. The village *Keba* is under intense pressure from the influence of money, power and the party politics. The instances of favouritism and partiality in the *Keba* decision are on the rising trend. The sense of unity and cooperation in the village is being slowly replaced by jealousy, envy, division and internal competition. Collectivism and cohesiveness, which was the basic characteristics of the rural areas, has gradually eroded. Hence, under such circumstances, the decision of the *Keba* is not always transparent and conducive to the social harmony and justice. There is every possibility of justice being doctored, delayed or denied. However, in spite of the declining level of egalitarian character of the *Keba*, almost all the leaders prefer to settle their dispute in the village *Keba* because, disputes when taken to the higher forum becomes complicated and expensive. The study further reveals that the emerging leaders have better understanding about the emerging realities; and the traditional leaders have relatively greater degree of reverence for the traditional *Keba*. Another perceptible change in the decision-making process is the diminished role of the elders. The majority of the respondents agreed that the educated could take better kind of decision. In the rapidly changing rural scenario, the decisions of the *Keba* is not necessarily guided by the customs and conventions alone, but on many occasions, the decisions are influenced by the other factors like modern concept of justice and equality, official norms, party interest, etc. Under such circumstances, the educated are likely to play a more effective role in the decision-making process. Our study further reveals that the decision-making process is more democratic in the traditional *Keba* when compared to the statutory panchayat because; there are greater instances of arbitrary decisions in the panchayat meetings. Most of the *Keba* decisions are taken through the consensus method, but in the panchayat, most of the decisions are taken through the majority. This is so, because, the *Keba* decision being the product of lengthy deliberation facilitates greater scope for consensus decision. But, in panchayat, the decision is more often influenced by the party interest and the governmental supervision. So, there is a greater chance of arbitrary and discretionary decisions in the panchayat. Though the consensus decisions seem to be the most appropriate, the majority of the leaders admitted that the majority decision is practically more reliable. Inspite of the certain difference in decision-making process between the traditional *Keba* and the statutory panchayat, they can influence one another or they are not totally independent from one another.

The emergence of leadership in the rural and tribal society is basically based on ascriptive factors. However, our study indicates that the primordial loyalties do not play as effective a role in the leadership formation in the Galo society anymore, though we cannot completely ignore the same. The traditional determinants of leadership have not been totally jettisoned though the trend is towards new direction in the pattern of leadership and authority in the village. As far our analyses, the parental position has important bearing on the emergence of leadership, because the majority of the respondent leaders' father held some position or status in the village. This finding subscribes to the proposition that 'the son inherit the father's quality' which is popularly accepted in the traditional Galo society. Further, the parental position has greater significance for the modern leaders. However, the leaders' fathers were basically poor in terms of monetary income though they might have been wealthy in traditional perspective. Almost all of them were agriculturist by occupation and it was their source of income too. So far our study is concern, the most important base of leadership is the personal achievement, followed by the party support and the family background. A person with good reputation of honesty and integrity and social service coupled with other positive qualities usually emerge as leader in the village in long run. The integrity and honesty is important not only for the emergence of leadership, but also a crucial factor, which determines the voting behaviour of the respondent leaders in the elections. The integrity of the candidate and the party factor usually determine the leaders voting behaviour in both the panchayat and the Assembly elections. The family, clan and the economic factor have very limited role in determining the leaders' political decision in the election. The study further reveals that the majority of the leaders' in-laws held some position in the society, which imply that the in-laws social position also contribute to the leadership formation. The substantial proportion of the respondent leaders admitted that they got support from the in-laws in acquiring and maintaining the present status. Thus, the socio-economic status of the in-laws has also bearing on the leaders' status though not instrumentally. The analyses further indicates that the traditional leaders who represent the village *Keba* are, ironically but slightly, more broad-based than the modern leaders who represent the democratic institution of the panchayat and the parties. However, our analyses could not clearly establish the influence of primordial loyalties in the leadership formation in a big way. The Galo being a classless society, the leadership rests with a collectivity of individuals in the village. The birth and descent does not necessarily determine the leadership formation because of the relative homogeneity of the society.

Bibliography

Ashraf, A.A., *Prehistoric Arunachal*, Directorate of Research, Govt. of Arunachal Pradesh, Itanagar, 1990.

Baden, B.H. Powell, *Indian Village Community*, Cosmo Publications, Delhi-6, 1972.

Bandyopadhyay, P.K., *Leadership Among the Mizos*, B.R. Publication Corporation, Delhi, 1985.

Bhargava, B.S., *Grassroot Leadership*, Ashish Publishing House, Delhi, 1979.

Bhattacharjee, J.B., *Proceedings of NEIHA* (7th Edition), Shillong, NEHU, 1986.

Bhattacharjee, J.B., *Sequences of Development in North East India*, Omsons Publications, New Delhi, 1989.

Bhattacharjee, T.K., *Alluring Frontiers*, Omsons Publication, Guwahati & Delhi, 1988.

Bhattacharjee, Tarun Kumar, *The Frontier Trail*, Eminent Printing Works, Calcutta-31, 1993.

Bhuyan, B.C., *Political Development of North East*, Vol. I, Omsons Publications, New Delhi, 1989.

Burns, J. MacGregor, *Leadership*, Ambika Publication, New Delhi, 1978.

Chattapadhyay, S.K. (ed.), *Tribal Institutions of Meghalaya*, Spectrum Publications, Guwahati, 1985.

Choudhary, D.S., *Emerging Rural Leadership in Indian State*, Manthan Publication, Delhi, 1981.

Choudhary, S. Dutta, *Gazetteers of India, Arunachal Pradesh, East Siang and West Siang Districts*, Govt. of Arunachal Pradesh, Itanagar, 1994.

Choudhary, D.S., *Rural Leadership in an Indian State*, Manthan Publication, Delhi, 1981.

Chowdhury, J.N., *A Comparative Study of Adi Religion*, Department of IPR, Shillong, NEFA, 1971.

Dai, Mamang, *Arunachal Pradesh—the Hidden Land*, Sky Prints Pvt. Ltd., New Delhi-48, 2000.

Dalton, E.T., *Descriptive Ethnology of Bengal*, Asiatic Society of Bengal, 1872.

Das, Gurudas, *Tribes of Arunachal Pradesh in Transition*, Vikas Publishing House Pvt. Ltd., New Delhi-14, 1995.

Desai, A.R., *Rural Sociology in India*, Popular Prakashan Pvt. Ltd., Bombay, 1969.

Dube, S.C., *Tradition and Development*, Vikas Publishing House Pvt. Ltd., New Delhi, 1990.

Dunbar, George, *Frontiers*, Omsons Publication, Guwahati & Delhi, 1932.

Dutta, Parul, *The Wanchos*, Directorate of Research, Govt. of Arunachal Pradesh, Itanagar, 1990.

Dutta, S. (ed.), *Study in History, Economy and Culture of Arunachal Pradesh*, Himalayan Publications, Delhi and Itanagar, 1997.

Ete, Tumpak, *Pume Dada Hoi Dada and Oyo Hei Ya*, Adi Folk Literature Research Centre, Along, Arunahal Pradesh.

Gassah, L.S., *Traditional Institutions of Meghalaya—A Study of Doloi and His Administration*, Regency Publications, New Delhi, 1998.

Haimendorf, Christoph Vonfurer, *Himalayan Adventure*, Sterling Publishers Pvt. Ltd., New Delhi, 1983.

Haimendorf, Christoph Vonfurer, *Tribes of India*, Oxford University Press, Delhi, 1985.

Horam, M., *Naga Polity*, B.R. Publishing Corporation, Delhi.

Judge, P.S. & Sharma, S.K. (ed.), *Dimension of Social Change*, Rawat Publications, Jaipur, 1997.

Kothari, R., *Politics in India*, Orient Longman Ltd., New Delhi, 1970.

Krech, David and others, *Individual in Society*, McGraw Hill Book Company Inc.

Lalini, V., *Rural Leadership in India*, Gyan Publishing House, New Delhi, 1991.

Manpong, C.P. and Das, M.N., *District Administration in Arunachal Pradesh*, Omsons Publication, New Delhi-27, 1993.

Mathur, K.S. (ed.), *Studies in Social Change*, Ethnographic and Folk Culture Society, U.P., Lucknow, 1973.

Mibang, T., *Social Change in Arunachal Pradesh*, Omsons Publication, Delhi, 1994.

Mishra, K.K., *Tribal Elites and Social Transformation*, Inter-India Publication, New Delhi, 1994.

Mishra, Kiran, *Women in a Tribal Community—A Study of Arunachal Pradesh*, Vikas Publishing House Pvt. Ltd., Delhi-14, 1991.

Mishra, S.N. and others, *Tribal Voting Behaviour*, Concept Publishing House, Delhi, 1982.

Mishra, S.N., *Political Socialization in Rural India*, Inter-India Publication, Delhi, 1980.

Mukherjee, B., *Political Culture and Leadership in India*, Mittal Publication, New Delhi, 1991.

Nag, C.R., *The Mizo Society in Transition*, Vikas Publishing House Pvt. Ltd., New Delhi, 1993.

Negi, Dev Singh, *A Tryst with the Mishmi Hills*, Tushar Publication, New Delhi, 1996.

Nyori, T., *History and Culture of the Adis*, Omsons Publications, Delhi, 1993.

Pandey, B.B., *Arunachal Pradesh—Village State to Statehood*, Himalayan Publication, Delhi & Itanagar, 1997.

Pandey, B.B., *Leadership in a Tribal Society*, Spectrum Publication, Guwahati, 1991.

Pandey, D.N., *Local Govt. in Arunachal Pradesh*, Himalayan Publishers, Delhi & Patna, 1995.

Pandey, Rajendra (ed.), *Modernization and Social Change*, Criterion Publications, Delhi, 1988.

Panigrahi, P.K., *Political Elite in Tribal Society*, Commonwealth Publishers, New Delhi, 1998.

Parmar, T.S., *Polyandry in the Himalayas*, Vikas Publishing House, Delhi, 1975.

Pathak, Manjushree, *Crimes, Customs and Justice in Tribal India—A Teleological Study of Adis*, Mittal Publication, New Delhi-59, 1991.

Pilania, G.P., *Leadership*, RBSA Publication, Jaipur, 1991.

Raha, M.K. & Coomar, P.C. (ed.), "*Tribal India*", Vol. II, Gyan Publishing House, New Delhi, 1989.

Raikar, Y.A. and Chatterjee, S., *Archaeology in Arunachal Pradesh*, Directorate of Research, Govt. of Arunachal Pradesh, Shillong, 1980.

Roucek, S. Joseph, *Social Control*, Affiliated East-West Press Pvt. Ltd., New Delhi.

Roy, B. Datta, *Emergence and Role of Middle Class in North East India*, Uppal Publications House, New Delhi, 1983.

Roy, Sachin, *Aspect of Padam-Minyong Culture*, NEFA, Shillong, 1966.

Samanta, R.K. (ed.), *India's North East—The Process of Change and Development*, B.R. Publishing Corporation, Guwahati, 1994.

Shah, Ghanshyam (ed.), *Social Transformation in India*, Rawat Publication, Jaipur, 1997.

Sharma, S.S., *Rural Elites in India*, Sterling Publication Pvt. Ltd., New Delhi, 1979.

Singh, Avtar, *Leadership Pattern and Village Structure*, Sterling Publishers Pvt. Ltd., New Delhi, 1973.

Singh, B.P., *The Problems of Change--A Study of North East India*, Oxford University Press, Delhi, 1987.

Singh, K. Suresh (ed.), *Tribal Situation in India*, Indian Institute of Advance Study, Simla, 1972.

Singh, Karnal (ed.), *Tribal Laws and Modern Legal System*, Himalayan Publisher, Patna, 1993.

Singh, R.S., *Rural Elites, Entrepreneurship and Social Change*, Rawat Publications, Jaipur, 1985.

Singh, U.K., *Arunachal Pradesh—A Study of Legal System of the Adis Tribes*, Vikas Publishing House, Delhi, 1991.

Srivastava, L.R.N., *The Gallong*, Directorate of Research, Govt. of Arunachal Pradesh, Itanagar, 1960.

Talukdar, A.C., *Political Modernization in Arunachal Pradesh in Sequences of Development in North East India*, ed. by J.B. Bhattacharjee, Omsons Publications, New Delhi, 1989.

Talukdar, A.C., *Political Transition in the Grassroots in Tribal India*, Omsons Publication, Guwahati and Delhi, 1987.

Tewary, I.N. (ed.), *Political System—Micro Perspective*, Anmol Publications, Delhi-51, 1986.

Thakur, Devendra (ed.), *Rural Development and Political Leadership*, Deep and Deep Publications, New Delhi, 1986.

Verma, B.M., *Rural Leadership in a Welfare Society*, Mittal Publication, New Delhi, 1994.

Vidyarthi, L.P. (ed.), *Leadership*, Asia Publishing House, Delhi, Bombay, Calcutta, 1968.

Vidyarthi, L.P. (ed.), *Tribal Development and Its Administration*, Concept Publishing House, New Delhi, 1981.

Vidyarthi, L.P. and Rai, B.K., *The Tribal Culture of India*, Concept Publishing Company, Delhi, 1977.

ACTS AND RULES

- The Assam Frontier (Administration of Justice) Regulation, 1945.
- The North East Frontier Areas (Administration) Regulation, 1954.
- Daying Ering Committee Report, 1965.
- The NEFA Panchayati Raj Regulation, 1967.
- The Inner Line Regulation of 1843.
- The Assam Frontier Tracts Regulation, 1914.
- Govt. of India Act, 1919.
- Govt. of India Act, 1935.
- Constitutional (Seventy Third Amendment) Act, 1992.
- The Provision of the Panchayats (Extension to the Scheduled Areas) Act, 1996.
- Arunachal Pradesh Panchayati Raj Act, 1997.

JOURNALS AND MAGAZINES

- *Arunachal News*, Directorate of IPR, Govt. of Arunachal Pradesh, Itanagar.
- *NEFA Information*, Directorate of IPR, NEFA Administration, Shillong.
- *RESARUN* : Journal of the Department of Research, Directorate of Research, Govt. of Arunachal Pradesh, Shillong & Itanagar.
- *ARSI*, Central Solung Festival Committee, Pasighat, Arunachal Pradesh.

Glossary

Abbala	:	Village Council of the Idu Mishmi.
Abhor	:	The present Adi tribe was called so.
Abotani	:	Common ancestor of the Galos.
Adam	:	Traditional disc and bowl; a valuable property.
Agam-Layap	:	Small ritual by which a marriage is consummated.
Ali or Opin	:	Title or Surname or Clan.
Ane-Donyi	:	Mother Sun—The Galos consider the Sun as God.
Areh	:	Rate or Price.
Buliang	:	Village Council of the Apatanis.
Donyi-Poloism	:	New religion of the Adis.
Emo	:	Arrow fitted with an iron point and grinded poison.
Gam	:	Village authority appointed by the government.
Gomin	:	A messenger to assist the Monpa Tsorgen.
Hurin-Namrin	:	A big ritual among the Galos in which the entire villager is invited to a feast.
Jikte	:	A prominent priest.
Jung	:	Village Council of the Sherdukpens.
Jung Me	:	Members of the Sherdukpen Village Council.
Keba	:	Village Council of the Galos (Adi).
Keba Abo	:	Village elders.
Kebang	:	Village Council of the Minyong-Padam group of the Adia.
Keden	:	A traditional friendship maintained throughout the generation.

Khaphua, Khapong, Khapo	:	Village Councils of the Tangsas.
Lako	:	A kind of fine or punishment wherein the *Keba* snatch a household item from a person who do not obey the *Keba* decision.
Mangma	:	Panel of assessors to assist the Monpa Tsorgen.
Mele or Razz	:	Village Council of the Akas.
Mokchup	:	Village Council of the Khamptis.
Neppe-Nyida	:	A kind of marriage in advance wherein the marriage is negotiated before the birth of the prospective couple.
Ngothun	:	Village Council of the Nockte.
Nyame Renam/ Ginam	:	Sexual relationship with the wife of endogamous clan brother.
Nyibuh	:	Priest.
Nyida Tanam	:	Marriage proposal.
Nyijik	:	Priest.
Nyiji-Nyira	:	Two broad divisions of the Galos but no more adhered to.
Nyikok	:	A prominent orator with knowledge about the tradition, precedents and customary laws.
Nyitom-Ponu	:	Traditional songs and dance.
Nyochi	:	Name of an ancestor.
Nyoi	:	Name of an ancestor.
Omeh Areh	:	Bride price.
Opo or Poka	:	Local wine popularly knows as *Apong*.
Pakbo	:	Male slave.
Pakne	:	Female slave.
Pedong Nane	:	Mother of all beings (Adi).
Polo	:	Moon.
Rutum	:	Influential and wealthy person.
Sitem	:	Clan brother of the same generation.
Tadok	:	Beads or traditional necklace.

Tamo	:	Poison trees or plants.
Thik Akhao	:	Village headman of the Sherdukpen.
Togu	:	A grand marriage celebration wherein number of mithuns are sacrificed.
Tsoblas	:	Representative of the Tsorgen in different villages.
Tsorgen	:	Chief of the Monpa Council.
Tso-Tsangzom	:	Village Council of the Monpas.
Uyi or Uyu	:	Deities.
Wancho-Wangcha	:	Council of Elders in Wancho Village Council.
Wangham	:	Wancho chief.

Index

W

Y